# Moral Agoraphobia

# Revisioning Philosophy

David Appelbaum
*General Editor*

Vol. 25

PETER LANG
New York • Washington, D.C./Baltimore
Bern • Frankfurt am Main • Berlin • Vienna • Paris

Kim-Chong Chong

# Moral Agoraphobia

## The Challenge of Egoism

PETER LANG
New York • Washington, D.C./Baltimore
Bern • Frankfurt am Main • Berlin • Vienna • Paris

**Library of Congress Cataloging-in-Publication Data**

Chong, Kim Chong.
Moral agoraphobia: the challenge of egoism/ Kim-Chong Chong.
p. cm. — (Revisioning philosophy; vol. 25)
Includes bibliographical references.
1. Egoism. I. Title. II. Series.
BJ1474.C47 171'.9—dc20 95-16202
ISBN 0-8204-2839-6
ISSN 0899-9937


**Die Deutsche Bibliothek-CIP-Einheitsaufnahme**

Chong, Kim-Chong:
Moral agoraphobia: the challenge of egoism/ Kim-Chong Chong.
–New York; Washington, D.C./Baltimore; Bern; Frankfurt
am Main; Berlin; Vienna; Paris: Lang.
(Revisioning philosophy; Vol. 25)
ISBN 0-8204-2839-6
NE: GT

Cover design by James F. Brisson.

The paper in this book meets the guidelines for permanence and durability
of the Committee on Production Guidelines for Book Longevity
of the Council of Library Resources.

© 1996 Peter Lang Publishing, Inc., New York

Printed in the United States of America.

# Contents

# Acknowledgments

Several friends and colleagues have provided criticisms, suggestions and also helped to proofread—Mabel Eickemeyer, Cecilia Lim, Alan Chan, John Williams, Chew Mun Yew, Charlene Tan, John Greenwood, Robert Stecker, Colin Davies, and especially John Kekes, who has also been a constant source of encouragement. Some criticisms and suggestions are acknowledged in the notes. This book originated as a Ph.D. thesis, submitted to the University of London, in 1983. My supervisor then was Peter Winch, to whom I owe an everlasting debt. My colleague and former Head of Department, Goh Swee Tiang, provided the friendly push which helped the project to be completed. Rosna Buang painstakingly wordprocessed several drafts. The care and integrity with which she approaches her work is, nowadays, rare.

Portions of the book have appeared elsewhere. The major part of chapter 2 originally appeared as "Ethical Egoism and the Moral Point of View," *The Journal of Value Inquiry* 26 (1992): 23-36. (© 1992 Kluwer Academic Publishers. Reprinted by permission of Kluwer Academic Publishers.) A large part of chapter 4 originally appeared as "Egoism, Desires and Friendship," *American Philosophical Quarterly* 21 (1984): 349-357. A version of chapter 5 originally appeared as "Impersonalism, Goals, and Sensitivity in Ethics," in a book which I edited, *Moral Perspectives* (Singapore University Press, 1992). I thank the publishers and editors for permission to publish the modified versions of these papers here.

I dedicate this book to my wife and daughter, Kathy and An Ho.

"People dare not—they dare not turn the page. The laws of mimicry—I call them the laws of fear. People are afraid to find themselves alone, and don't find themselves at all. I hate all this moral agoraphobia—it's the worst kind of cowardice." (André Gide, *The Immoralist*).

# Chapter One

# Introduction:
## Moral Agoraphobia and Perspectives

Much of contemporary moral theory defines morality in terms of rationality. These definitions confine morality within a narrow, enclosed space. The "moral agoraphobia" of the title of this book refers to this state of affairs and suggests an abnormality.

Egoism, as discussed by contemporary Anglo-American analytic philosophers, seems to fall outside these well-defined boundaries, almost by default. It is as if the boundaries are drawn with the specific task of excluding egoism as a matter of course. The moral theorists have therefore not taken seriously the question, What if their attempts to exclude egoism fail? What then has been shown about morality?

The answer is—nothing. The rationalist moral theorists are in a paradoxical position when egoism can be shown to meet the criteria of rationality put forward to exclude it, and hence becomes "morality." We are left with no clue as to how satisfying certain criteria of rationality could make egoism a "morality." This is precisely what is abnormal—how could anything so enclosed as criteria of rationality be said to constitute "morality?"

It should not be thought that we ought then to look for tighter (and therefore even more enclosed) criteria of rationality. Instead, the confined space of this "morality"—this agoraphobic way of looking at morality and the obsession with rationality—hides the possibility of different moral perspectives which are much wider than what the moral theories (prescriptivism, contractualism, cognitive psychotherapy, etc.) have been able to countenance.

At the same time as it discusses the possibility of different perspectives, part of the task of this book is also to examine the concept of a perspective and the role it plays in helping us understand the nature of morality. But first, we have to show that egoism can fully meet the criteria of rationality put forward by the various moral theories.

The challenge of egoism to moral philosophy is not new. The classic discussion is to be found in Book II of Plato's *The Republic*,[1] where Glaucon describes the nature and origin of justice as a compromise between suffering from the injuries others inflict on one, and being able to injure others with impunity. But if one had the absolute power to do as one liked, e.g., with the magical Gyges' Ring, it would be the height of stupidity for one to act justly or morally. Adeimantus supplements this with a description of conventional beliefs and customs which show that the ordinary person believes that it pays to be just, and that this is why he should act justly. Ever since this poser to Socrates to provide an alternative account of morality, egoism has provided a challenge to the adequacy of definitions and theories of morality. As Peter Winch has aptly noted, "Glaucon's challenge has haunted moral philosophy ever since...."[2]

Contemporary definitions of morality and moral theories have been tested by the possibility of egoism being an ethical principle. This possibility is given the name, "ethical egoism." I argue in chapter 2 that ethical egoism succeeds as a moral principle, within the terms of a conventional definition of morality as social co-operation. Morality accommodates much more than the conventional or social definition allows for.[3]

A discussion of examples (Menalque in *The Immoralist,*[4] and Zorba in *Zorba the Greek*[5]) show how and under what circumstances, the limits of morality can be extended. This involves a description of Menalque's and Zorba's perspectives, and how these could be moral perspectives. What emerges is not the notion of ethical egoism as an alternative and rival guide to action, i.e. morality constituting one such guide while egoism another, but the possibility of various moral perspectives.

The picture of egoism as constituting a non-moral guide is given by prescriptivism[6] and contractualism,[7] the "moral games" referred to in the title of chapter 3. The egoist is regarded as someone having to hide his real self from others, to derive the benefits of social co-operation while seeming to co-operate. In other words, he is deceitful, exploitative and manipulative (a non-moral guide becomes manifestly immoral). The essential question is, however, whether he is rational.

I argue that the egoist, as defined within the framework of prescriptivism, fully plays the game of prescriptivity and universalizability. And philosophers who have argued that he is irrational, in the context of contractualism, have underestimated the possibilities of deception. What makes their argument appear more convincing than it should is the way the question has been posed, i.e. whether one can, in the deceitful way envisaged, stay *outside* of morality. If, as we would all agree, it is either too costly or impossible to do so, the egoist is asked to consider the more rational possibility of "entering" or living within the bounds of morality.

Whether it makes sense to talk of staying outside the bounds of morality,[8] or entering it, an egoist like Rosamond in George Eliot's *Middlemarch*[9] shows that one can deceive others and yet not be shunned by them. It is the community of Middlemarch which nurtures the egoism of Rosamond. Social and personal relationships are complex enough to allow such an egoism to flourish. Rosamond, who fits the philosopher's description of the egoist as deceitful, manipulative and exploitative, operates *within* the social co-operative matrix, not outside it.

Rosamond is not a philosophical invention, while ethical egoism is. As we have said, the latter has been spawned by moral theorists to serve as a heuristic challenge to definitions and theories of morality. In fact, it succeeds in meeting the criteria set by them. But it is an indication of their inadequacy that we are no nearer to an understanding of morality, once we see that the ethical egoist meets these criteria. Some proponents of ethical egoism have tried to remedy this by showing how ethical egoism itself provides a satisfying (but not, as we shall see, a satisfactory) moral theory.

Perhaps I may preface it with a brief anecdote, as such a theory strikes a chord with many, philosophers and non-philosophers alike, who speak of an "enlightened self-interest." A diplomat informed me that the people of a certain country were generally very disagreeable, except those he met on official business, who saw to his needs and took care of him. But, he went on, they did this only because they knew that it was *quid pro quo*—that if they visited his country, they expected the same would be done for them. This, he concluded, is "what you philosophers would call, enlightened self-interest."

The philosophical account which I discuss in chapter 4 is more subtle.[10] Instead of being deceitful and manipulative, the ethical egoist is said to be actually capable of having a genuine and direct concern for the welfare of others and, as such, is also not precluded from having close personal relationships. Indeed, it is assumed that the egoist—in fact any fully rational person—would best maximize his interests, if he had such relationships. In this way, ethical egoism, as a moral theory, supposedly provides an attractive way of explaining the concern which one may have for another person. If one has a genuine concern for another, one cannot but have a desire for his welfare. And insofar as the rational act is that which maximizes personal utility, one is, in satisfying this desire, doing what one rationally ought to do. That is, in satisfying a desire for the welfare of another, by acting to secure his welfare, one is doing no more and no less than maximizing personal utility or self-interest. This is said to apply to all cases of (genuine) concern.

Against this, I show how concern for another is different from a concern with the (rational) maximization of personal utility. I also analyze the conception of love and friendship implicit in the theory of ethical egoism expounded here. Under this conception, it is for the sake of gaining certain goods and benefits that one enters into a relation of "love and friendship." But, I argue, a true relation of love and friendship does not come about through a conscious and persistent concern for gaining such "goods and benefits" (e.g. feelings of warmth and security). Instead, that such "benefits" exist is an indication of there being a close personal relationship, in which care and concern is shown for the other person.[11]

This argument is extended to include a critique of contemporary Humeans[12] who argue in various ways for the ultimacy of motivational considerations in action, based on some desire-state. I argue that one should distinguish among the desires. I provide a phenomenological description of what constitutes genuine concern as opposed to, say, a desire to purchase a piece of property (with non-unique characteristics). The two are of a different logical order in that the former is "non-transferable," whereas the desire to purchase a piece of property, if unsatisfied, could still be satisfied by being transferred elsewhere.

Understanding the non-homogeneity of desires also enables us to understand the notion of a perspective. Borrowing some examples from Derek Parfit,[13] I show how it is that talk of "desire" itself is inadequate to understand the significance of certain projects for the individual concerned, to see how something might be meaningful for the agent, or how it is that he or she *must* perform a certain task. Talk of a desire or choice in these contexts is out of place. Thus, someone's dedication to scholarship is not merely described as a desire for scholarship, but is to be described in terms of the meaning and the importance of the activity for her. Described in this way, what is important to her is no longer a matter of desire. It is not as if what she desires were quite arbitrary. Instead, her desires are constrained by what she sees as important and what she is committed to, in terms of this importance. In a certain case, as discussed, this might even mean a renunciation of life itself.

Here, we have already begun the task of examining the concept of a perspective in morality. Chapter 5 goes beyond the usual discussions of ethical egoism, where the challenge is to fulfil criteria of rationality, to ask the question, What area of human sensitivity does egoism offend against even though it may be rational? The key to understanding this is to note that the characteristics of the impersonal point of view, with which morality is often identified,[14] could be shared by an egoist. As we shall see, Rosamond employs these impersonal considerations in the successful execution of her egoism. Far from detecting what is morally offensive about egoism, impersonalism, instead, could be said to underlie it.

It might be protested that this constitutes an abuse of the formal criteria and therefore it is not the criteria themselves which form an egoistic perspective. But this raises an interesting point. Criteria do not apply themselves, it is moral agents who apply them—from a perspective.

The example of Dorothea in the same novel shows how a concern for another may be personally grounded, i.e. concern is shown for her husband, Casaubon, within the context of a narrative history[15] of her relationship with him. The concern which she expresses is the culmination of a process of moral growth. Any attempt to give formal criteria or impersonal reasons for this concern distorts its sense and significance as a moral perspective.

The contrast of Rosamond and Dorothea shows how it is that moral growth may be possible in one person but not in another. Given this possibility, the person, one could say, constitutes a certain perspective. And this in turn, could play a role in what one would or would not recognize as a moral resolution. I test this idea against the claim that there is in principle an objectively established impersonal point of view which necessarily governs the perspective of any agent, if he or she is fully rational.

This is discussed in chapter 6, with a focus on Dorothea's dilemma whether to promise Casaubon to complete his project, a *Key to All Mythologies* (which, by all accounts, is worthless), after he dies. From the impersonal perspective, the "obvious" and most rational solution is to promise and break the promise after Casaubon's death. This is, however, not Dorothea's perspective. We have to understand her decision to promise in the context of her relationship with Casaubon. She had committed herself to him and cannot break the relation of trust which she believes exists between them. It is conceivable, as Dorothea herself seems to recognize, that someone else in a relevantly similar situation and with a similar relation (however unlikely this may be), might take the rational solution outlined earlier. But this only shows a different perspective and not that in a case like this, there is an impersonal perspective that necessarily governs how she—indeed, anyone—should act.

The point was made earlier that any conception of morality, defined in a certain way, is capable of application according to different perspectives. This might be sharpened by the realization that there is no perspectiveless conception of morality which serves as a ruler against which all actions are to be judged. In this regard, there are two theories which may be considered to either directly or indirectly endorse the perspectiveless view. These are the "cognitive psychotherapy" of Richard Brandt,[16] and the "view from nowhere" of Thomas Nagel.[17]

Brandt's definition of rational action as "fully informed" action fails, because it is too idiosyncratic. Thus, I argue, I may have made a mistake in a certain case because I was not fully informed. It does not follow that I was not thereby acting rationally, at the time when I made the mistake. In any case, full information does nothing to indicate *how* I may view the information. Brandt's emphasis on informed action leaves out the all-important perspective of the agent, which serves to evaluate the facts. Without the agent's particular perspective, full information is perspectiveless, and hence ineffectual.

Nagel's "view from nowhere" is not a coherent underpinning for the kind of concern which Dorothea evinces for others when she reminds herself not to cling to (what she sees as) selfish complaints, and to involve herself in helping others. Stated like this and given the narrative context, there is a sense in which she may be said to be acting "impersonally." It is worth repeating the passage about Dorothea which I quote in chapter 6, here:

> She opened her curtains, and looked out towards the bit of road that lay in view, with fields beyond, outside the entrance-gates. On the road there was a man with a bundle on his back and a woman carrying her baby; in the field she could see figures moving—perhaps the shepherd with his dog. Far off in the bending sky was the pearly light; and she felt the largeness of the world and the manifold wakings of men to labour and endurance. She was a part of that involuntary, palpitating life, and could neither look out on it from her luxurious shelter as a mere spectator, nor hide her eyes in selfish complaining. (MM 846).[18]

Clearly, this is a description of a perspective and not as it might appear, a description of the scenery from Dorothea's window. If this is an impersonal perspective, it shows that "impersonal" is neither "perspectiveless" nor from "nowhere."[19] The fault lies with Nagel's relocation of the self to a point outside the world, a kind of metaphysical underpinning which supposedly makes for objectivity. And, we might add, with reference also to Brandt (against whom the example is directly used, in chapter 6), it is not *what* Dorothea sees that is at issue here and therefore not a matter of having full information, but *how* she sees—a matter of perspective.

Any attempt to divest ourselves of a perspective is itself a perspective. There is no pure, unsullied self which stands independently of any perspective. We stand somewhere. We act from some perspective. This is what we learn from the example of Michel, in Gide's *The Immoralist*, which I discuss in chapter 7. Michel is confused when he thinks that he can divest himself of all moral distinctions and look for the pure, unsullied self, which he thinks can be found outside the constraints imposed by these distinctions. His search leads to self-destruction, not purity.

There are echoes of Nietzsche in Michel's immoralist quest. Alexander Nehamas[20] interprets Nietzsche as holding the philosophical view that there are, essentially, no moral facts. It is a contextual perspective which gives value to the facts. Nietzsche shows that all events are homogeneous, all moral distinctions are conditioned by perspective and the moral is, in essence, identical with the immoral. There is no good and evil.

I argue that although morality can serve an ideological purpose, e.g., in moral education, conceptions of good and evil arise for the individual through various ways, not necessarily connected with such indoctrination. Thus, someone may develop integrity through his engagement in and dedication to, some activity. Morality, in this sense, is not an external imposition as it might be for someone who merely pays lip-service to the rules inculcated in him, for fear of the consequences of disobedience. We all have to operate through a moral language and whether we view this as an imposition, modify it or make it our own in some way, depends on the kind of person we are—the kind of perspective we have.

In short, I clarify the nature of ethical egoism in order to show, contrary to the philosophical consensus, that it can be a coherent ethical principle. This leads to a discussion of contemporary moral theories such as prescriptivism, contractualism, cognitive psychotherapy and Nagel's "view from nowhere." Underlying all these theories are various conceptions of rationality. I argue that not only have some of them been unsuccessful in banishing egoism from the moral field, but that furthermore, they all fail in one way or another, to give an underpinning to morality. The nature of morality is not to be understood in terms of these theories of morality. Instead, it is better understood by attending to the possibility of various perspectives.

I make much use of literary examples, particularly from George Eliot's *Middlemarch* and André Gide's *The Immoralist*. It is my conviction that a close attention to good literary examples serves as a healthy antidote to philosophical theories about morality, which often distort the realities and the complexities of moral life. It may also interest literary scholars to know how well George Eliot fares, when put against the moral philosophers I have discussed.[21]

In conclusion, it must be said that my task is a limited one, as described in the preceding paragraphs. Perhaps more could be done. It might be said, for example, that I have not discussed Aristotle, and his conception of the good life. This would involve an examination of happiness and eudaimonia, the roles of various virtues, the different forms of friendship, the conception of a plan of life, and the contingencies of life (what has lately been described as "moral luck"[22]). All this would require more than I am inclined to give.

My own inclination, as may be gathered from the conclusions in this book, would be to argue that any philosophical conception of the good life is, in itself, one perspective on life and cannot claim to give a rational or theoretical underpinning to everyone, to lead that life.

# Notes

1 Plato, *The Republic*, translated by Desmond Lee (Harmondsworth: Penguin, 1955).

2 Peter Winch, "Moral Integrity," in *Ethics and Action* (London: Routledge and Kegan Paul, 1972), p. 173.

3 This is the definition given by William Frankena, *Ethics* (Englewood Cliffs, N.J.: Prentice-Hall, 1963). See also Frankena's "The Concept of Morality," in *The Definition of Morality*, edited by G. Wallace and A.D.M. Walker (London: Methuen, 1970).

4 André Gide, *The Immoralist*, translated by R. Howard (New York: Bantam Books, 1976).

5 Nikos Kazantzakis, *Zorba the Greek*, translated by Carl Wildman (London: Faber and Faber, 1961).

6 The theory usually associated with R.M. Hare in his three books: *The Language of Morals* (Oxford: Clarendon Press, 1952), *Freedom and Reason* (Oxford: Clarendon Press, 1963), *Moral Thinking* (Oxford: Clarendon Press, 1981). Hare himself does not directly discuss ethical egoism. But the prescriptivist argument against ethical egoism is developed by George Carlson, "Ethical Egoism Reconsidered," *American Philosophical Quarterly* 10 (1973).

7 I shall discuss in particular, David Gauthier, *Morals By Agreement* (Oxford: Clarendon Press, 1986).

8 See Rush Rhees, "On Knowing the Difference between Right and Wrong," in *Without Answers* (London: Routledge and Kegan Paul, 1969), for a discussion of contexts in which it would make sense to talk of "opting out of morality."

9 George Eliot, *Middlemarch* (Harmondsworth: Penguin, 1976).

10 The account as given by Richard Brandt, "Rationality, Egoism and Morality," *Journal of Philosophy* 69 (1972), and Jesse Kalin, "Two Kinds of Moral Reasoning: Ethical Egoism As A Moral Theory," *Canadian Journal of Philosophy* 5 (1975).

11 Michael Stocker, "The Schizophrenia of Modern Ethical Theories," *Journal of Philosophy* 73 (1976), makes a similar point.

12 By "contemporary Humeans," I refer to the anti-Kantian stance in contemporary moral philosophy, that argues for the primacy of desire in any reason for action—any action must have an end based on some prior desire, and reason is instrumental in the achievement of that desire. Historically, this may be traced to David Hume's assertion in *A Treatise of Human Nature*, Book II, Part III, Section III, that "Reason is, and ought only to be the slave of the passions, and can never pretend to any other office than to serve and obey them." Philippa Foot and Bernard Williams, in certain of their writings, may be regarded as contemporary Humeans. See Foot, *Virtues and Vices* (Berkeley: University of California Press, 1978), chapters 10-13, especially chapter 11, "Morality As A System of Hypothetical Imperatives." See Williams, *Moral Luck* (Cambridge: Cambridge University Press, 1981), especially chapter 2, "Moral Luck." Also Williams, *Ethics and the Limits of Philosophy* (London: Collins, 1985), especially chapter 10, "Morality, the Peculiar Institution." Williams' *Shame and Necessity* (Berkeley: University of California Press, 1993), moves away, I think, from a Humean stance, toward a perspectival analysis. (See note 21, chapter 6, where I give a brief explanation of this.) Hume's moral psychology is deeper than may be assumed by the simple dichotomy between reasons and desires. See Stephen Holmes, "The Secret History of Self-Interest," in *Beyond Self-Interest*, edited by Jane J. Mansbridge (Chicago: University of Chicago Press, 1990).

13 Derek Parfit, *Reasons and Persons* (Oxford: Clarendon Press, 1984). Parfit is not a Humean in the sense defined in note 12, above. But I show that his discussion of desires, in regard to the examples mentioned, is similarly inadequate.

14 I have in mind especially the Kantian and the utilitarian (or consequentialist) views of morality. Both Kantian and utilitarian elements are combined in R.M. Hare, *Moral Thinking* (Oxford: Clarendon Press, 1981).

15 I borrow this term from Alasdair MacIntyre, *After Virtue* (Notre Dame, Indiana: University of Notre Dame Press, 1984).

16 Richard Brandt, *A Theory of the Good and the Right* (Oxford: Clarendon Press, 1979).

17 Thomas Nagel, *The View From Nowhere* (New York: Oxford University Press, 1986).

18 All page references to *Middlemarch* in the book shall henceforth be given in parentheses after the quotations, under the abbreviation MM.

19 My use of "impersonal" to describe Dorothea's perspective here may be somewhat forced. As my colleague Alan Chan has commented, if he looks at the "same" view (from Dorothea's window), he may complain that those people are ruining his view! But I think this states the point I wish to make very nicely.

20 Alexander Nehamas, *Nietzsche: Life As Literature* (Cambridge, Massachusetts: Harvard University Press, 1985).

21 Some recent discussions of George Eliot as a moral theorist: M.C. Henberg, "George Eliot's Moral Realism," *Philosophy and Literature* 3 (1979). Carol Gould, "Plato, George Eliot and Moral Narcissism," *Philosophy and Literature* 14 (1990). I do not discuss George Eliot as a moral theorist, and as such, I do not discuss her novels as a whole, nor do I discuss a range of characters from her novels or from a particular novel. Instead, I work relevant examples, primarily those involving Dorothea and Rosamond from *Middlemarch*, into the philosophical arguments which I present, because they are particularly pertinent to the arguments.

22 See Thomas Nagel, "Moral Luck," in his book *Mortal Questions* (Cambridge: Cambridge University Press, 1979), and Bernard Williams, "Moral Luck" (see note 12 above).

## Chapter Two

## Exploring Moral Limits:
## Egoism as Social Outlaw

In the philosophical literature, there have been various attempts to elucidate the sense in which egoism can be "ethical" or "moral."[1] This has given rise to the name, "ethical egoism." To the layman at least, this sounds paradoxical. How can something be both egoistic and ethical at the same time? This paradox is in fact taken at face value by some philosophers who use it as a heuristic illustration of what morality means and the limits which it encompasses. In this chapter therefore, I shall discuss the possibility of egoism as a moral principle.

The writers I shall presently discuss sometimes refer to ethical egoism as a moral theory. Strictly speaking, however, they are actually discussing the coherence or intelligibility of it as a moral principle vis-a-vis certain pictures of morality. Not surprisingly, the so-called "theory" comes out rather poorly—little or no attempt has been made in their discussions to articulate a theory to justify the principle, and this is apt to make it arbitrary or absurd as a *moral* point of view. The examples I shall give to show how and why someone might come to adopt such a principle will to some extent remedy this, while a discussion of ethical egoism as a moral theory emerges in chapter 4.

In what follows, I shall consistently refer to ethical egoism as a principle, although unavoidably, the term "theory"[2] will be used by the writers discussed. Beginning with definitions of ethical egoism, I shall look at reasons that have been given against its being a moral principle and argue that they do not succeed. This is largely because of misconceptions and misinterpretations of ethical egoism. These arise from a narrow and unilluminating conception of morality, usually referred to as "the moral point of view"—as if there were no other moral point of view. An appreciation of ethical egoism as a moral principle arises out of a critique of "the moral point of view."

### Definitions of Ethical Egoism

Ethical egoism has been defined as the view that "each and every man ought to look out for himself alone,"[3] "everyone ought to concern himself with his own welfare alone,"[4] "my sole duty is to promote my own interests exclusively,"[5] and "everyone ought exclusively to pursue his own interests."[6]  In these formulations, ethical egoism advocates the exclusive pursuit of one's own interests.

It is generally acknowledged that the "exclusive" pursuit of one's own interests need not be interpreted to mean performing only that course of action which would result in benefiting the egoist solely.  That is, given two courses of action which may benefit the egoist but one of which will benefit another as well, the egoist is not claiming that he ought to perform that action which would benefit himself alone.  Rather, what he does is determined by the thought of whether it would, all things considered, be in his overall interest to perform one action instead of another.  This does not preclude him from doing things which would benefit another so long as it is in his overall interest to do so.

While it is clear that there is no necessary incompatibility between the egoist's interests and others', an exclusive concern with self-interest may still give the impression that the egoist will always disregard others' interests.  Some definitions of ethical egoism in fact stress this point, that a *disregard* for the interests of others is itself a defining characteristic: "Universal egoism maintains that everyone (including the speaker) ought to look after his own interests and to disregard those of other people except in so far as their interests contribute toward his own,"[7] "we should try to maximize our own intrinsic good and ignore everyone else's,"[8] and, "according to the ethical egoist, a person is always justified in doing whatever is in his own interests, regardless of the effect on others."[9]

Such definitions notwithstanding, the point is more simply that the egoist must always regard his own interests as overriding.  In other words, ethical egoism should not be reduced to the idea that "everyone ought to act in his own interests," leaving unspecified the degree to which the egoist ought to carry out his pursuit of self-interest.  As such, it might be indistinguishable from say, classical utilitarianism, which also sanctions the pursuit of self-interest, at least to the extent that the general interest is maximized.  The overridingness of self-interest is brought out clearly by the following two, essentially similar formulations:

(1)  (x) (y) (x ought to do y if and only if y is in x's overall self-interest).[10]

(2)  (x) (y) (x ought to do y if and only if y maximizes x's utility).[11]

As one philosopher has noted, these indicate two conditions which are unique to ethical egoism. First, that the agent ought always to act in his own interests and second, that he ought only to act in his own interests.[12] While accepting both formulations as definitive of ethical egoism, the question arises of the sense in which ethical egoism may be said to be a moral principle.

### Unease about "Ethical" Egoism

One major debate in this connection has been whether the principle of ethical egoism can be consistently prescribed and universalized.[13] As this forms an issue in itself, I shall discuss it in the next chapter. For now however, we should note that prescriptivism does not rule out any ultimate principle as being a moral principle, so long as it passes the test of prescriptive universalizability. On prescriptivist grounds, no absurdity is attached to the possibility of ethical egoism being a moral principle.[14]

But there are other views. William Frankena[15] for instance, has observed that "prudentialism or living wholly by the principle of enlightened self-love just is not a kind of *morality*." The prudential should not be confused with the moral point of view which is "*disinterested*, not 'interested,'" otherwise the meaning and function of morality would be obscured.

A central difficulty, as Frankena sees it, is what the ethical egoist would have to say about second and third person moral judgments, for instance those used in giving moral advice and adjudicating moral disputes. According to Frankena, the consistent egoist is committed to the tenet that anyone making such judgments should do so on the basis of his own advantage. Thus, for instance, in giving moral advice to someone, the advisor should go by what is to his own advantage. Taken as such indeed, ethical egoism can hardly "serve as an acceptable basis for this important part of morality," but it is doubtful if it should be construed in this way.

The problem with this view is that it would turn ethical egoism into a meta-ethical principle purporting to define morality in a way that is (absurdly) at odds with how it is ordinarily used and understood. But, as Frankena himself recognizes, ethical egoism is a normative theory or principle.[16] Thus, the ethical egoist is not precluded from giving moral advice, he knows what it means to make moral judgments, and is not trying to give these a peculiar meaning of his own.

However, is the egoist not logically obliged to give (moral) advice only on the basis of his own advantage? Well, there could be occasions when his interests may be tied up, in various ways, with the advice that he gives. This means that his motives may not (entirely) be "pure," not that he is confused about or trying to change the meaning of moral terms. On other occasions, however, he may give advice or make judgments without being *obliged* to do so on the basis of his own advantage.

Another interpretation of ethical egoism is likewise ill-supported. Both Edward Regis, Jr. and W.D. Glasgow hold that ethical egoism "embodies or presupposes a principle of positive significance, the equal autonomy of moral agents."[17] According to Glasgow, "To say that [everyone ought to look after his own interests] is to grant at least that there are other human beings who are autonomous."[18] Further, "There is an implication that all autonomous (or potentially autonomous) individuals are ends-in-themselves."[19] Regis extends the implications of this last statement of Glasgow's: if one acknowledges that all individuals are ends-in-themselves, one at the same time acknowledges that they have certain rights, e.g. the right of self-determination, to take self-interested action and to enjoy the results of such action. This means also, the acknowledgement of a duty to respect these rights. It follows that there are constraints to egoistic conduct—one may not perform self-interested actions which may harm others. Consequently, ethical egoism has to be interpreted to mean, not that one ought always and only to act self-interestedly, since this is not consistent with constraints on action harmful to others, but that one has "no unchosen moral obligation or duty to serve the interests of others," while pursuing one's well-being and happiness.[20]

Underlying Regis' interpretation is an uneasiness in accepting the usual interpretation of ethical egoism. As he says, "no definition of ethical egoism will mark out a successful moral theory unless it is consistent with the possibility of constraints against self-interested action harmful to others."[21] Going further than Frankena whose complaint against egoism is that it is non-moral, Regis construes the egoist as immoral—he is said to lack constraints to his actions, and this implies harming others.[22] He therefore attempts to transmute ethical egoism into a morally orthodox position incorporating a principle of respect for (the rights of) others. Beside making ethical egoism no longer recognizable, Regis' interpretation is unwarranted insofar as there is no discussion of the contexts in which it might be true to say that the egoist's self-interested actions may harm others, what constitutes "harm" in these cases, and whether any action leading to harm may be *justifiable*.

Glasgow, on the other hand, is led to the above interpretation of ethical egoism because of a failure to appreciate fully the way in which the ethical egoist may accept the universality of reasons. He assumes that recognizing the universality of reasons (and hence others' autonomy) requires at the same time that one should accept certain reasons for action, however disastrous it may be for oneself.[23]  But this is questionable, as we shall see in the debate over prescriptivism, in the next chapter.  If the egoist is not logically committed to prescribe his own disadvantage or harm while accepting universalization, then we need not accept this Kantian interpretation of ethical egoism as embodying a principle of respect for the autonomy of all moral agents.

## The Social Definition of Morality

I shall now examine a certain social definition of morality which underlies much of the criticisms against ethical egoism in the last section. The aim here is to explicate further the sense in which ethical egoism is a normative principle of action. I shall focus on the definition given by Frankena, which succinctly captures a view of morality held by many, the so-called "moral point of view."  As we shall see, this in no way rules out ethical egoism as a normative principle.  On the contrary, it forms the background against which the normative nature of ethical egoism has its sense.

Frankena[24] is concerned to stress that morality is a "social enterprise," and not an individual invention for personal guidance. Thus, while there are rules within morality which govern interpersonal relations, it is important to note that many such rules can be personally generated, e.g. "My rule is to smile first," and morality cannot be equated merely with these.  Morality is social in its origins, sanctions, and functions. "Like one's language, state, or church, it exists before the individual, who is inducted into it and becomes more or less of a participant in it, and it goes on existing after him." Furthermore, it is "an instrument of society as a whole for the guidance of individuals and smaller groups."

From this standpoint, morality makes demands on individuals independently of their wishes.  Initially at least, these demands are external although individuals may eventually become their "spokesmen" through a process of internalization. But even then, the demands remain impersonal for they are still not merely the individuals' own demands, nor directed only at themselves. And should the individuals come to disagree with these demands, "they must still do so from the moral point of view which has somehow been inculcated into them." Reiterating the contrast between morality and prudence, and while recognizing that prudence itself could be a moral virtue, Frankena stresses that it is not characteristic of the moral point of view "to determine what is right or virtuous wholly in terms of what the individual desires or what is to his interest."

Nonetheless, while Frankena sees morality as a social enterprise, he cannot deny that at the same time, there is an important individualistic aspect to morality. Thus, he says, "morality fosters or even calls for the use of reason and for a kind of autonomy on the part of the individual, asking him, when mature and normal, to make his decisions...and even stimulating him to think out the principles or goals in the light of which he is to make his decisions." In other words, the individual may come to discover for himself, on rational grounds, the principles which are to guide his life.

This points to a crucial tension in Frankena's account of morality which ultimately supports, rather than undermines, egoism as a moral principle. To begin with, it is not entirely clear where the limits of autonomy lie once it is allowed that the autonomous individual may work out for himself, on rational grounds, the principles which are to govern his life. Thus, one could argue that it is precisely the "moral point of view" as outlined which makes ethical egoism attractive, or gives it an impetus, as a guide to action. For the fact that morality, as socially defined, exists before the individual, and that it will continue to exist after him gives him no reason why, as a thinking individual, he ought to accept it. The analogy of morality with the institutions of the state and the church reinforces this attitude. For it is often the case that the rules laid down by these institutions are those which a self-determining individual ought to question. The reference to language, on the other hand, holds a different implication. That is, morality is something which governs the individual's communication with others, or even enables him to communicate with others. As such, it is something he cannot do without. But it is left imprecise just what the connection between language and morality is, i.e. in what sense the individual has to accept morality as socially defined, just as he has to accept a language.

An important point to note is that the ethical egoist can accept that morality, as ordinarily conceived, is something he cannot do without. This merely means he cannot afford a life without moral rules (as against rules of his own) to guide social interaction and in particular, to resolve conflicts of interest. Even so, one should not assume that morality resolves all such conflicts—it could be argued for instance, that a defining feature of morality is the irresolvability of conflicts at certain levels and in certain contexts.[25]

But if we assume that the egoist would prefer a life-situation in which rules govern conflicts of interest, and morality, broadly speaking, defines such a situation, the point is that he does not accept this situation as having intrinsic value, i.e. he does not accept the common interest of all the members of society as having a value in itself. Instead, what has intrinsic value for him is *his* interest. The argument against accepting ethical egoism as a moral principle or theory, on the other hand, assumes a conception of morality in which the common interest has intrinsic value.[26] Hence, the so-called "moral point of view," which takes for granted the equal consideration of interests.

Frankena could reply that the features of the social morality which he describes are constitutive features of *any* morality and hence definitive of it. The moral point of view is, as such, not just a particular point of view but definitive of any particular moral theory or principle. Ethical egoism, defined as the principle that one ought to perform some action if and only if it is to one's overall self-interest to do so, clearly falls outside the moral point of view.

The answer to this is that the definition of morality as encapsulated in "the moral point of view" is both too restrictive and unhelpful in understanding the tensions within the various strains of the concept of morality itself. Thus, we have already seen evidence of an important tension in Frankena's account above, when he talks of the individualistic aspect of morality, which allows for development of the mature and autonomous individual who may decide for himself the goals and principles which are to guide his life. To say that such development takes place "within" morality, however, is just what is unhelpful and obscure, as we would like to know what sort of development is possible here. And if one were to call it a *moral* development, it would be unhelpful to reiterate the moral point of view as described by Frankena. Worse, chances are that such a development could contradict this point of view. As we have seen, some of the features of this moral point of view are precisely what the rational autonomous individual would argue against adopting, e.g. the goals and rules laid down by certain institutions, the idea of the common interest as being intrinsically valuable, etc.

The tension in Frankena's own account of moral development is revealing. He accepts the general account of the stages of development given by some social psychologists, in which we come to internalize a set of rules which were originally imposed on us, or inculcated as habits, and acquire a "conscience" or "superego." At the same time, Frankena stresses that we can move from this "rather irrational kind of inner direction" toward "a more rational one in which we achieve an examined life and a kind of autonomy, become moral agents on our own, and may even reach a point when we can criticize the rules and values of our society...." He tries to resolve this tension by claiming that we may do so "without leaving the moral fold."[27]

Enough has been said of the way in which the metaphor (for that is what it amounts to) of the "moral point of view" sets limits to morality. These limits do not serve to illuminate the concept of morality. Instead, they obscure the possibility of various moral perspectives, as revealed but not exploited in Frankena's account. We shall explore this possibility in the next section.

In fairness to Frankena, he has given other reasons elsewhere for ruling out egoism from the moral field.[28] According to him, the necessary conditions for a morality include not just prescriptivity, universalizability and the overridingness or supremacy of some principle. In addition, the principle must "concern the relations of one individual to others," and furthermore, it must "involve or call for a consideration of the effects of (one's) actions on others (not necessarily all others), not from the point of view of his own interests or aesthetic enjoyments, but from their own point of view."

Frankena's worry is that without the last two stipulations, no distinction is left between prudentialism, aestheticism, some forms of religion, immoralism, and "pure egoism" on the one hand, and morality on the other. Another worry is that the wider definition (consisting of the first three stipulations) would be misleading, given that the term "morality" confers a social importance and legitimacy. Society would have no moral justification for punishing any individual who acts conscientiously on his own principle or action-guide, which calls on him to act in a way which "does not consider others in any important way." In the final analysis, these objections to "pure egoism" etc. being a morality rely on the fact that "the function of morality is not just to serve as a supreme action-guide but to make possible some kind of cooperation or social activity between human beings."

However, Frankena's definition of morality is not as narrow as it seems, for he explicitly allows the Nazi action-guide to qualify as a moral code (although not necessarily a valid one), even though it ignores the rights of Jews. This is because "it did require an individual to consider other Germans." But if such arbitrary "consideration" and "social-cooperation" are allowed, then Frankena cannot disqualify egoism as a moral code, since it is possible for the egoist to have a consideration for others and to cooperate with them socially. He too, like the Nazi, could consider the interests of a circle of people whom he may relate to.

In the final analysis, Frankena's main objection is that the egoist looks at others' interests from the perspective of his own interests. This fundamental tenet of egoism disqualifies it from being a morality, and any attempt to build it into the definition of morality must therefore be rejected.

This is where the reference I have made in the beginning to ethical egoism as a moral theory is relevant, in answering Frankena's objection. Frankena is referring to prudentialism, immoralism, and "pure" egoism, where out of a seeming consideration for others, someone does something from the motive of his own interests. A person who acts characteristically in this way is, of course, open to moral censure, and it is no excuse to claim that he is following his own action-guide. Instead, such a claim merely shows his perniciousness. On the other hand, a theory of self-interest which claims to be a moral theory would require an enlarged or enlightened conception of self-interest, such that a consideration for the interests of others, or a concern for them, would be constitutive of self-interest. Nothing rules out this possibility, least of all the mere assertion that morality and self-interest are incompatible. This assertion may make sense in the contexts just mentioned, but these do not rule out a philosophically justified link between morality and self-interest. Reference has also been made to ethical egoism as a normative principle. This shall be discussed further, in the next section.

**Extending the Limits**

From what has been said so far, it would be wrong to conclude that ethical egoism has been *justified* as a moral principle. I have merely tried to clarify the sense in which ethical egoism could be a normative principle. But certainly, the lack of examples in discussions on ethical egoism has obscured this possibility. In what contexts would a principle of egoism arise? What reasons could someone have for adopting a principle of acting always and only on self-interest? The following two examples may throw some light on these questions. Contrary to "the moral point of view" already discussed, they show how egoism could fall squarely within morality and indeed, highlight certain important aspects of it.

Consider, first, the following protest of Menalque, a character in André Gide's novel, *The Immoralist*. Menalque, in a conversation with Michel, expresses unambiguously his contemptuous impatience with the moral distinctions and reservations which people make (although he doesn't specify what these are). For his own part, Menalque lays claim to nothing but his own nature and asserts that the pleasure that he takes in an action is "my clue to its propriety." Upon Michel's answer that this kind of attitude could take him too far, Menalque replies that he means it to, and further remarks:

> If only these people around us could be convinced. But most of them believe they get nothing good out of themselves except by constraint; they're only pleased with themselves when they're under duress. If there's one thing each of them claims not to resemble it's...himself. Instead he sets up a model, then imitates it; he doesn't even choose the model—he accepts it ready-made. Yet I'm sure there's something more to be read in a man. People dare not—they dare not turn the page. The laws of mimicry—I call them the laws of fear. People are afraid to find themselves alone, and don't find themselves at all. I hate all this moral agoraphobia—it's the worst kind of cowardice. You can't create something without being alone. But who's trying to create here? What seems different in yourself: that's the one rare thing you possess, the one thing which gives each of us his worth; and that's just what we try to suppress. We imitate. And we claim to love life.[29]

And later, when Michel states that he detests a man of principles, Menalque agrees, saying that "You can't expect any kind of sincerity from him...." Here, we have at least two persons who share similar thoughts and feelings (Menalque inspires Michel's own hidden thoughts and feelings), agreeing on a creed which insists on the assertion of self ("...the pleasure I take in an action is my clue to its propriety"), as against the "submergence" into morality. The "moral agoraphobia" that Menalque refers to, we may say, includes some of the constitutive features of the social definition of morality earlier described. Chief among these, perhaps, is the idea that one is inducted into and must accept certain institutionalized goals and rules. This is because morality is a social enterprise and like one's language, state, or church, exists before the individual and is thus an instrument for the guidance of its members. Menalque, on the other hand, is asserting the autonomy of the self, against the acceptance and imitation of "ready-made" models of action. The justification for this assertion of self is, conceptually speaking, a moral one. Menalque's remarks carry the conviction that people who unquestioningly bow to the dictates of morality, guided by its rules and principles without thinking for themselves and without asserting themselves, are cowardly, imitative, and insincere.

Suppose it is denied that Menalque is making a *moral* criticism—it might be argued for instance, that terms like "imitative" and "cowardly" are not necessarily moral (as against non-moral) ones. After all, isn't the point he is making essentially that appeals to morality and moral considerations can stifle individual expression and creativity? Menalque is not merely making the point that people do not think for themselves, for someone may make the effort to think and still conclude that he ought to act on moral principles. Rather, he is saying that they should, in the face of all kinds of moral prohibitions and inhibitions, self-assertively "find themselves." A man may, to his own detriment, be too hemmed in by (the fear of) moral criticisms and judgments, for this would, more often than not, prevent him from doing things he might enjoy or find valuable and worthwhile to himself. And these projects need not be morally valuable or morally worthwhile.

The first point, in answer to this objection, is to deny that terms like "imitative" and "cowardly" are non-moral. It is a vice to be imitative and cowardly in certain contexts and as such, these terms are used not just to record a fact, but as moral condemnation. The second point is that the limit of what constitutes moral judgment cannot be set independently of the circumstances under which the judgment arises. In this regard, Menalque's criticisms can be accommodated within the moral realm instead of being regarded as denying morality altogether.

One important characteristic of morality is the fact that tensions are created out of the conflicting demands that may arise in the life of an individual. A man may, for instance, think of giving rein to his artistic impulses, and this may involve giving up a respectable job and impoverishing his family.[30] If he goes ahead with this "impulse," he may be branded by people around him as irresponsible. Whether he accepts this judgment as justified or not depends on the extent to which this is merely an "impulse," rather than something which is based on an adequate assessment of his own capabilities and the implications of his intended move for himself and his family. Such a reply on his part would of course not mean that moral considerations hold no validity at all for him, but show instead that he is trying to answer what he considers to be an unjustified moral charge.

Another answer he might possibly give and which would be more in line with Menalque's convictions, is that he is always going to let self-interest reign, and not care about charges of "irresponsibility." It is more important, he may claim, that he should develop his capabilities and "find himself." Assuming that this is not a mere whim on his part, and he does not claim "finding oneself" as a moral justification, the most that this shows is that moral considerations are not always overriding. In other words, where moral reasons conflict with non-moral ones, the former are not always held to be more important and decisive. (I exclude cases of "weakness" here.) But the fact that moral considerations are not necessarily always overriding is not something which invalidates the claims of morality as a whole, in all situations. Neither is this fact something which is inherently denied by the idea of morality itself. It may be that morality is held to be always overriding by a particular moral point of view, in the sense that one ought always to perform one's duty *and* that there are no self-interested duties. (It is another matter whether this is a justifiable point of view to hold.)

However, it may now be objected that once you allow the possibility of self-interested reasons having the decisive edge over moral reasons in any one situation, you also allow that they may always overcome moral reasons.[31] And this is precisely what is paradoxical about so-called "ethical" or "moral" egoism—that it takes a vantage point *outside* of morality and thus it is an incompatible non-moral alternative, or even completely an amoralistic position.[32]

Once again, however, it is no use drawing a line here. One lesson to be learnt from the above discussion is how idle the word "morality" is, once we see the various circumstances and ways in which it has an application. That is, it really does little or no work once these circumstances are described.[33] Perhaps the next example will help us here. It comes from Kazantzakis' *Zorba the Greek*. The following diatribe is by Zorba, after his idealistic companion and boss, the narrator of the story, has tried to preach a form of communism (communal-sharing) to their fellow-workers:

'Man is a brute...A great brute. Your lordship doesn't realize this. It seems everything's been too easy for you, but you ask me!...If you're cruel to him, he respects and fears you. If you're kind to him, he plucks your eyes out.

'Keep your distance, boss! Don't make men too bold, don't go telling them we're all equal, we've got the same rights, or they'll go straight and trample on your rights; they'll steal your bread and leave you to die of hunger....'

'But don't you believe in anything?' I [the narrator] exclaimed in exasperation.

'No...only in Zorba. Not because Zorba is better than the others; not a little bit! He's a brute like the rest! But I believe in Zorba because he's the only being I have in my power, the only one I know. All the rest are ghosts....'

'What egoism!' I said sarcastically.

...I admired him for being so strong, for despising men to that extent, and at the same time wanting to live and work with them.[34]

Given the harsh, nasty and brutish conditions existing in many places in the world, there are many who would share Zorba's mistrust of his fellow-men. For someone like Zorba, the appeal to morality and moral considerations such as that others' interests (ought to) count equally with his, together with the constraints on action which this implies, will sound hollow, and he would mock all talk of this kind. Nevertheless, he may be said to have a normative position, one which is derived from his experiences with men—the cruelty, and the injustice, of which they are capable.[35] If he were led to articulate a principle such as, "one ought always and only to act in one's own interests," it is the moral background against which it comes to be held, that goes to justify it as a normative principle. The principle of ethical egoism, in other words, is not a matter of arbitrary choice,[36] it is the background against which it is formed which may justify its claim as a moral principle.

In a critique of an earlier paper[37] on which this chapter is based, Wim J. van der Steen[38] has argued that Zorba's position, though universalizable, does not justify ethical egoism. He puts it this way:

We are dealing either with a universal principle that remains to be justified, or with a principle which, though justified, is non-universal because it is person-relative.

Alternatively, Chong's line of reasoning could be taken to show, more sensibly, that acting along the lines prescribed by ethical egoism is justified *in circumstances of a particular kind* (cf. the "background" mentioned by Chong). This would leave us with a thesis which is justified and universal, but clearly less general than unqualified egoism as originally defined by Chong.

Either way ethical egoism as an overarching doctrine remains to be justified. Chong implicitly assumes, mistakenly so, that justifiability is preserved under universalization.[39]

Van der Steen allows that Zorba's position is a universalizable one, but doubts its generality. This would not make it fit the definitions of ethical egoism borrowed from Brandt and Kalin. But the original problem was to make sense of "ethical" egoism, i.e. to clarify the sense or senses in which egoism may be a normative ethical position, as distinguished from a meta-ethical theory trying to provide an absurd re-definition of morality. My discussion of examples has served several purposes. One was to show how egoism could develop as a normative principle against certain conventional assertions of the authority of social guides, described as "the moral point of view"—as if there were no other moral perspectives. Another was to question the "overridingness" of morality. A third, more relevant to van der Steen's discussion, was to show how the lack of examples in discussions of ethical egoism serves to obscure the possibility of ethical egoism as a normative position. As stated earlier, nothing has been said in this regard to justify ethical egoism either as a principle or a moral theory. My examples were not designed to do either, but to justify its claim as an "ethical" principle. In other words, against claims that ethical egoism is either absurd or arbitrarily chosen, I argue that the discussion of examples allows us to understand (the motivations behind) egoism as a normative position. I have not attempted to argue that ethical egoism is justified because it is universalizable.

Brandt's and Kalin's definitions of ethical egoism, on the other hand, do presuppose moral theories which attempt to justify the principle. These shall be discussed in chapter 4. But this is a different issue from the intelligibility of ethical egoism as a moral principle. The significance of this may be better appreciated if we remind ourselves that there have been many attempts by contemporary moral theorists to define morality, and egoism is seen as being challenged—and in turn challenging—these definitions, especially those which draw an intimate connection between morality and rationality. Van der Steen, referring to my remark that prescriptivism does not rule out any ultimate principle from being a moral principle so long as it passes the test of universalizability, comments that "this rash dismissal of problems with universalizability is not satisfactory."[40]  I shall deal immediately with prescriptivism and universalizability in the next chapter.  As we shall see, the success of egoism in meeting criteria of rationality put forth by prescriptivism is extremely paradoxical.

# Notes

1 I use "ethical" and "moral" interchangeably.

2 For a distinction between "principle" and "theory," see chapter 4.

3 Donald Emmons, "Refuting the Egoist," *Personalist* 50 (1969), p. 311. This and the following definitions are all cited in Edward Regis, Jr., "What Is Ethical Egoism?" *Ethics* 91 (1980).

4 Emmons, op. cit., p. 312.

5 John Hospers, "Baier and Medlin on Ethical Egoism," *Philosophical Studies* 12 (1961), p. 10.

6 Bernard Williams, *Problems of the Self* (Cambridge: Cambridge University Press, 1973), p. 250.

7 Brian Medlin, "Ultimate Principles and Ethical Egoism," in *Morality and Rational Self-Interest*, edited by David Gauthier (Englewood Cliffs, N.J.: Prentice-Hall, 1970), p. 57.

8 John Hospers, *Human Conduct* (New York: Harcourt Brace Jovanovich, 1972), p. 141.

9 James Rachels, "Egoism and Moral Scepticism," in *Moral Philosophy: An Introduction*, edited by Jack Glickman (New York: St. Martin's Press, 1976), p. 168. See also Richard Brandt, "Rationalism, Egoism and Morality," *Journal of Philosophy* 69 (1972), p. 689 and Jesse Kalin, "In Defense of Egoism," in *Morality and Rational Self-Interest*, edited by David Gauthier, op. cit., p. 79.

10 Kalin, op. cit., p. 65.

11 Brandt, op. cit., p. 687.

12 Regis, Jr., op. cit., p. 59.

13 See George Carlson, "Ethical Egoism Reconsidered," *American Philosophical Quarterly* 10 (1973). Also, J.A. Brunton, "The Devil is Not a Fool or Egoism Re-Visited," *American Philosophical Quarterly* 12 (1975).

14 For a discussion of prescriptivism, see the works of R.M. Hare cited in note 6 of chapter 1.

15 William Frankena, *Ethics* (Englewood Cliffs, N.J.: Prentice-Hall, 1973). What follows summarizes his views on ethical egoism in pp. 17-20 of his book.

16 Ibid., p. 17, where ethical egoism is discussed in the context of normative theories.

17 As stated in Regis, op. cit., p. 61.

18 W.D. Glasgow, "The Contradiction in Ethical Egoism," *Philosophical Studies* 19 (1968), p. 83. Quoted in Regis, op. cit., p. 61.

19 W.D. Glasgow, "Metaphysical Egoism," *Ratio* 12 (1970), p. 80.

20 Regis, op. cit., pp. 61-62.

21 Ibid., p. 61.

22 I thank Alan Chan for making me see more clearly the different forms of "unease" between Frankena and Regis.

23 Glasgow, "Metaphysical Egoism," op. cit., p. 83.

24 Frankena, *Ethics*. I summarize his account of "The Nature of Morality" in pp. 5-8 of his book.

25 As pointed out to me originally by Colin Davies. See Alasdair MacIntyre, *After Virtue* (Notre Dame: University of Notre Dame Press, 1981), p. 6: "The most striking feature of contemporary utterance is that so much of it is used to express disagreements; and the most striking feature of the debates in which these disagreements are expressed is their interminable character."

26 The two conceptions of intrinsic value are stated by Jesse Kalin, "On Ethical Egoism," in *American Philosophical Quarterly Monograph Series, Monograph No. 1: Studies in Moral Philosophy*, edited by

Nicholas Rescher (Oxford: Basil Blackwell, 1968), p. 39.

27 Frankena, *Ethics*, p. 7.

28 Frankena, "The Concept of Morality," in *The Definition of Morality*, edited by G. Wallace and A.D.M. Walker (London: Methuen, 1970), especially pp. 155-159 which I summarize below. See also his "Recent Conceptions of Morality," in *Morality and the Language of Conduct*, edited by Hector-Neri Castaneda and George Nakhnikian (Detroit: Wayne State University Press, 1965).

29 André Gide, *The Immoralist*, translated by R. Howard (New York: Bantam Books, 1976), p. 66.

30 As in Bernard Williams' example of Gauguin in his paper, "Moral Luck," in *Moral Luck* (Cambridge: Cambridge University Press, 1981). Williams describes the case of a creative artist, "who turns away from definite and pressing human claims on him in order to live a life in which, as he supposes, he can pursue his art." Williams explores and upholds "the claim that in such a situation the only thing that will justify his choice will be success itself." See pp. 22-23.

31 John Kekes discusses some interesting possibilities of conflict between moral and non-moral values in *The Morality of Pluralism* (New Jersey: Princeton University Press, 1993). See chapter 9, "Some Moral Implications of Pluralism: On There Being Some Limits Even To Morality," p. 178: "All things considered, agents may put love, beauty, creativity, and so on, ahead of the common good in many contexts. When they do that, they might act immorally, and yet they might also act reasonably. If the all-things-considered point of view were the same as the moral one, we could not express this thought, and we would thus deprive ourselves of an important possibility in life." See also Susan Wolf, "Moral Saints," *Journal of Philosophy* 79 (1982).

32 Dan Brock, "The Justification of Morality," *American Philosophical Quarterly* 14 (1977), p. 71, refers to egoism as "the principal non-moral alternative to morality among systems of practical reasoning." According to R.W.K. Paterson, "The conscious egoist

stands forward as the complete amoralist." *The Nihilistic Egoist, Max Stirner* (London: Oxford University Press, 1971), p. 261. John Rawls states that "although egoism is...not irrational, it is incompatible with...the moral point of view. The significance of egoism philosophically is not as an alternative conception of right but as a challenge to any such conception." *A Theory of Justice* (London: Oxford University Press, 1972), p. 135.

33 Wittgenstein, *Philosophical Investigations* (Oxford: Basil Blackwell, 1968), §132: "The confusions which occupy us arise when language is like an engine idling, not when it is doing work."

34 Nikos Kazantzakis, *Zorba the Greek*, translated by Carl Wildman (London: Faber and Faber, 1961), p. 57.

35 A possible criticism here is that when conditions are barbaric, morality has no foothold, because it makes superhuman claims on people. The answer to this is that this only shows human frailty, not that the nature of morality is as say, Frankena has described. I thank John Kekes for this comment.

36 As claimed by Medlin, "Ultimate Principles and Ethical Egoism," op. cit.

37 K.C. Chong, "Ethical Egoism and the Moral Point of View," *The Journal of Value Inquiry*, 26 (1992).

38 Wim J. van der Steen, "Egoism and Altruism in Ethics: Dispensing with Spurious Generality," *The Journal of Value Inquiry*, 29 (1995).

39 Ibid., pp. 33-34.

40 Ibid., p. 33.

# Chapter Three

# Moral Games:
## Prescriptivism and Contractualism

Prescriptivism and contractualism are "games" because of the rules devised to mark rationality. These rules provide a competitive format. In prescriptivism, the egoist is asked whether he is prepared to consider transgressions against his own interests, just as he is prepared to transgress against others'. In contractualism, the egoist is asked to consider the extent to which he can hope to (successfully) deceive others.

The prescriptivist critique assumes that the symmetrical relation between the egoist and his opponents requires that he should logically *allow* the harming of his interests. I argue that on the contrary, symmetry allows the egoist to resist any such attempt. Contractualism, on the other hand, underestimates the possibilities of deception.

## The Prescriptivist Framework

In the following discussion, ethical egoism is taken as the principle that "Everyone ought to act in his own interests, regardless of the interests of others." Similar to the unease mentioned in the last chapter, there may be something odd about this. For there does not seem to be anything "ethical" or "moral" about a principle which advocates acting according to one's own interests, regardless of the interests of others. The answer is that egoism has been used in this "ethical" formulation as a heuristic device, to test the application of two (professedly) central and formal features of morality, viz. prescriptivity and universalizability.[1]

Prescriptivity highlights the close connection between making or accepting a moral judgment, and *acting* on that judgment. The test of sincerely holding a *moral* judgment is whether one is prepared to assent to an imperative, "Do X" (and a singular prescription "Let me do X") if, having held or agreed that "One ought to do X," the occasion arises to do X.[2]

One's prescriptions are universalizable. Having made or accepted a moral judgment, one is logically obliged to make a similar judgment about another situation with relevantly similar circumstances.[3]

Given this framework, can egoism be universalized? Consider the following criteria of rationality:[4]

(1)   Efficaciousness—an act is rational if on the basis of given information, it offers optimal prospects of achieving its objectives.

(2)   Consistency—a rational decision must not involve any logical flaw in its calculation.

(3)   Reasoned or Principled—the sense in which an act is based on a "principle of action," which expresses an evaluative (though morally neutral) judgment of the form: "When in a situation of type C1...Cn, the thing to do is X." Its irrational counterpart is that range of actions that are based on wants which make no claim to being universalizable in the sense implied by the definition.

The third criterion is the primary one. The universalization of egoism brings a further question, whether the egoist thwarts his purpose of maximizing self-interest. If so, then he violates the other two criteria.

In an early paper on "Ultimate Principles and Ethical Egoism" which set the tone for much subsequent discussion on ethical egoism, Brian Medlin argues that the egoist is committed to universalizing and promulgating his doctrine. Insofar as we believe that someone should do so and so, "we have a tendency to induce him to do so and so."[5] The egoist is said to have incompatible desires because he wants both himself and others to win, despite a clash of interests. But no expression of incompatible desires could ever serve as an ultimate principle of conduct.

Jesse Kalin has questioned Medlin's assumption that we have a tendency to "induce" someone to do what we think he ought to do. Citing examples of competition, he argues that believing one's opponent ought to make certain moves does not commit one to *wanting* their occurrence.[6] George Carlson has counter-argued that Kalin's egoist is insincere for he "not only *wants* two different things for himself and others, but *believes* that two different states of affairs ought to obtain with respect to each (in his own case, a successfully negotiated egoism; in the case of others, a frustrated egoism)."[7]

Without as yet joining the debate, we should comment that Carlson's argument seems poor. The egoist's success cannot be held against him. Others too may succeed but it is not up to him to ensure this. All that is required is to allow a similar mode of *action* to others, and "success" is hardly an "action" in this sense.

J.A. Brunton[8] has remarked that "sincerity" is out of place here. The issue is not whether the egoist is immoral, but the intelligibility of egoism as a rational guide. The asymmetry of the egoist's attitude is not in dispute, but how we are to handle it. Brunton calls this attitude a "double-think." For example, an army commander may say of an opposing general that "He 'ought' never to have attacked us on the left flank," and in the same breath, also, that "He did just as he ought [no inverted commas], attacking us on the left flank. He's won the battle for us." Brunton elaborates:

> ...we are *contrasting* the sense of "ought" which relates to a hypothesis (if he knows his game, chess, war) and that which relates to the genuine desires of the egoist. Putting the matter in general terms; since, in a competitive game, one wants one's opponent to lose, any putting oneself in his place, taking his point of view, must be subordinated to the desire that he make the wrong moves, that he ought to do from the Egoist's point of view what he ought not to do from his own.[9]

Brunton concludes that the above three criteria of rationality are met. The egoist's "double-think" is efficacious, any contradiction is merely apparent, and the egoist may be said to have a "principle of action." All this still depends on a weak sense of universalizability. Brunton reiterates however, that "to insist on a strong sense of belief which impels the Egoist to approve his principles 'in a promulgatory, self-defeating way' (Carlson, p. 29) again does nothing more than insert a moral sincerity into one's analysis which has no place at the level at which it is introduced."[10]

But note that Brunton makes too easy a transition between "want" and "ought." Although I may want to beat my opponent, that would not, surely, warrant my saying that he truly *ought* to make (from his perspective) inferior moves. This reveals a weakness in both Brunton's and Kalin's positions, in that they have inadequately met the challenge to show in what sense the egoist's principle may be fully prescriptive but not contradictory.

It is undeniable that believing one's opponent ought to do certain things in order to win, does not amount to wanting him to win. These beliefs *anticipate* the opponents's moves so as to frustrate them, not *prescribe* them (unless it be a friendly, non-competitive game). The question of prescribing simply does not arise in a competition.

While Kalin and Brunton correctly deny that universalizability, purely as a condition of rationality, has anything necessarily to do with wanting others to do as one does, their arguments rely too heavily on the competitive analogy.   Consequently they fail to bring out the full implications of universalizability *in conjunction with* the logic of prescription.

The actual question is how can egoism be rational and *a fortiori*, an ethical principle, under the framework of universalizability and prescriptivity?  The asymmetry of the egoist's "double-think" described by Kalin and Brunton certainly violates this framework.  Must the egoist not be prepared, for instance, to prescribe his own harm, should the tables be turned on him?  It would seem that only then is symmetry preserved, under the rules of the ethical game.

### Fanatical Symmetry:  Playing the Game Fully

Let us clarify this through first briefly recounting R.M. Hare's example of the Nazi and the Jew.[11]  In holding that "All Jews ought to be persecuted," the Nazi is logically obliged to accept the singular prescription, "Let me be persecuted," were he to discover that he is of Jewish origin (this is to be imagined).  Hare holds that the Nazi is rational if he accepts this consequence, but few people are that fanatical.[12]

In *Moral Thinking*, Hare puts the case in terms of "preferences." Universal prescriptivism poses a dilemma for the fanatic.  Either he admits that his preferences do not outweigh his victims', or else he claims that his are so strong and unalterable that they will continue to prevail. In the former case, "if he fully represents to himself the stronger preferences of the others, he will come to have preferences of his own that, were they he, he should not suffer as he is proposing to make or let them suffer.  But then he will abandon his fanatical line of action and the universal prescription which requires it."[13]

We may apply this reasoning to the egoist, offering him two alternatives on the appropriate occasion.  He should either give up his egoistic principle or accept that his interests be transgressed against, whatever the consequences.  But this last point betrays the fault in the argument, and presents the egoist with a third and more realistic option. Realizing that when he acts against the interests of others they have every right to resist or retaliate, and that it would only be stupid or weak of them not to (attempt to) do so, he is just as entitled to resist a similar action against him.[14]

What the egoist should be represented as saying in the argument therefore is that he ought to act against the interests of another, without at the same time believing (absurdly) that the other party should consent. Thus, when he is placed in a similar position, he has every right to say, implicitly, "Let me resist, if I can," and not simply, "Let my interests be transgressed against." What has significantly been left out of the latter prescription is the implicit proviso, "...if they (my antagonists) are able to do so." Without this proviso the prescription reflects a penitent attitude, which is gratuitous to the argument. The egoist is merely committed to agreeing that others are *entitled* to act against him.

This symmetrical relation has the following advantages. Given that either party may resist the other's action, such resistance is compatible with the use of a fully prescriptive "ought." As such, the egoist is not Hare's amoralist, defined as one who either refrains from making moral judgments, or who only makes judgments of moral indifference.[15] Furthermore, not only is consistency preserved, due consideration is also given to prudence.

The prescriptivist poser to the egoist, whether he is prepared to prescribe his policy, is perhaps thought to have some force because of the unwarranted assumption that he cannot tolerate transgressions against his interests. But need the egoist, as a rational person, think that in each and every case, he must succeed in furthering or protecting his own interests? Surely not, for this would be an irrational basis upon which to work, beside importing a needless anxiety into his temperament. The egoist can consistently hold the following three beliefs: (a) that he ought to maximize his interests, (b) that others too, ought to do so (and he may prescribe that they do so), and (c) that at times, he may not succeed in furthering or protecting his interests. The objection that he cannot maximize his interests as a result of holding these beliefs again implies that he must believe he shall always win, which is unrealistic.

## Particularity and the Individualistic Axiom

So far, my arguments have kept closely to the prescriptivist framework. But it is time to question if one should be constrained by this at all. In admitting that his explanation of the egoist's asymmetrical position may not entirely satisfy Carlson, Brunton revives a much earlier argument of his own.[16] He argues that the "individualistic axiom," viz., "I am I (and it is in my interest to do x)" may, depending on one's point of view, be taken as a reason for action, *and*, at the same time, be regarded as no such reason. He puts the issue thus:

To state the question once more:  how can an enlightened Egoist appreciate an impartial, universalistic point of view to the extent that he admits it to be a rational point of view to hold, whilst, at the same time, he, himself, ultimately rejects it, arguing that for himself and similar minded persons the Individualistic Axiom is the reason for doing so?  I would argue that an ambiguous attitude towards mere particularity (I being myself, this being this particular occasion, etc.) is not only excusable, but, on the contrary, the most natural attitude to adopt.[17]

According to Carlson, for instance, it cannot be regarded as rational for anyone to cite the axiom as a reason for discriminative action since (as Brunton paraphrases it), "any *exceptional* treatment of, or attitude towards a particular person is always reiterable for others.  That is, *anyone* has equal reason, if it be a reason at all, to regard his own case as special, in that we are all in peculiarly intimate relationship to ourselves."[18]

Brunton's response to this line of argument is that:

In one sense a man's concern for a particular situation is very much related to that situation and to himself.  A man waiting to be hanged, whilst he admits that it would be just as terrible for another human being in an identical situation, has reason, in a very real sense, to be more concerned about his own situation than about an imagined replica.  He is concerned, that is, about a particular eventuality, not about a general description of it...I am arguing that one *can* regard one's particularity as an extra reason or consideration for discrimination, not that one must.[19]

It is unclear what Brunton means when he says that one "*can*" rather than "*must*" take one's particularity as an "extra" reason for discrimination.  This seems to dodge the question whether one's particularity *is* a reason for action, and perhaps he still feels embarrassed about the force of the objection that the individualistic axiom is not a justifiable reason.

Brunton's other remarks in the last quotation above however, are worth some consideration.  From any agent's (and not just the egoist's) perspective, one's own interests, projects and concerns have an (overriding) importance which it may not have for others.  This, I gather, is the sense of Brunton's remark, that "a man's concern for a particular situation is very much related to that situation and to himself." It ought to be clear however, that it is not merely the agent's *wanting* his own interests to be satisfied, or that these are *his* interests, which make it rational for him to pursue them. Rather, the full satisfaction of one's own interests is something which it is intelligible for *anyone* to want. And although not everyone may want to satisfy his own interests to the extent that the egoist does, it is not unintelligible for the latter to lay such stress on the satisfaction of his interests.

Thus while it may be true that what is a reason for one is logically open to others, this in no way affects the point just made, that someone may quite rationally consider his own interests, projects and concerns as overriding. (But although what is a reason for one must be logically "open" to others, it does not follow that it "must" also be a reason for others, as I shall argue in chapter 6). While doing so, he recognizes that others too, may think similarly. To argue that the rationality of egoism lies elsewhere than in prescriptive universalizability, is not to deny that egoism is universalizable. Instead, it is to give egoism its exact logical due.

**Contractualism**

Another theory which is challenged by egoism is contractualism.[20] The following general point has already been made in relation to prescriptivism. Criteria of rationality which stand independently of, and which are supposedly central to, morality, can be met by egoism. This is the risk which any moral theory takes in specifying such criteria. Thus, although contractualism provides a *moral insight* into the fact that morality involves co-operative constraints, it at the same time attempts to ground this insight externally, in terms of the maximization of self-interest. But the provision of an independent, rational justification attempts too much. For if one already possesses a moral understanding of the need for co-operation, there is no requirement for this justification. On the other hand, if the justification for moral understanding relies on independent factors such as the fact that one cannot successfully deceive others into thinking that one is co-operating with them, then whether one accepts the justification may depend on the extent to which this is true. The person who thinks he can successfully deceive others, or who is already doing so, has no reason to limit his self-interested acts. In other words, he is acting rationally through his deception, *and* maximizing utility.

Contractualism sees morality as the result of an agreement among rational, self-interested individuals. The agreement is to accept certain terms of co-operation, such that each individual would maximize his personal utility. The choice is between non-co-operation, where no one is well off, and co-operation such that everyone is better off. Following Thomas Hobbes, a hypothetical state of nature may be posited where, given that there are no rules to govern interaction and the concern of everyone is with self-preservation, life is "solitary, poor, nasty, brutish, and short."[21] The agreement to follow some set of rules to govern interaction is a rational move, not only for self-preservation, but also to attain the greater benefits of civilization. As Kurt Baier has put it, morality is an arrangement which allows all individuals to "maximize satisfaction and minimize frustration."[22]

Although it is easy to see that agreement to co-operate will maximize both social and personal utility, the problem for contractualism has always been whether it is rational for the individual to consistently conform to the agreement. It might be more rational to violate the agreement occasionally, when personal utility would be better maximized. There are situations where this may not lead to the collapse of the whole co-operative arrangement and others may be unaware of one's violation. How then does the group ensure compliance?

**The Game of Deception**

David Gauthier's recent answer expands upon an implicit point made by Hobbes.[23] By definition, an egoist, no matter how "enlightened" about his long range interests, is basically an exploiter who is morally unstable —he is ever-ready to break commitments. In other words, he is unreliable. Others, observing this, will tend to exclude him from co-operative activities. The character of the egoist means that he loses out on opportunities for the full maximization of his interests. A more rational choice, according to Gauthier, is to opt for morality or moral reasoning—to constrain one's egoistic tendencies by changing one's character into one which others can trust, and enter into co-operative ventures.

This argument assumes it is very unlikely that one can hide one's real character. Another conspicuous premise is the possibility of changing one's character. While change is sometimes possible, it is taken for granted that this can come about through a purely rational appreciation of long-run benefits. Not only is this doubtful, it also fails to consider what really constitutes moral growth. But let us focus on the first assumption, about the unlikely prospect of deceiving others.

In this regard, the most salient aspect of Gauthier's argument is the premise that we are all more or less "transparent" or "translucent" to others, and that "opacity" is most unlikely, or else unprofitable.[24] The distinctions among these are drawn in terms of the chances of a person's character or disposition being correctly identified by others. Thus, one is *transparent* if and only if others can always determine one's character, *translucent* if and only if others have more than an equal chance of correctly identifying one's character, and *opaque* if and only if others have merely an equal chance of correctly identifying one's character. The most realistic assumption is said to be that of translucency. Transparency and opacity, on the other hand, are not regarded as real options. In addition, being opaque renders one a bad risk to others, when they consider whether to include one in their co-operative ventures. Opaque persons will therefore have reason to make themselves more open or translucent to others.

But the assumption that we are translucent and therefore cannot easily deceive is too quick. Often enough, a large gap exists between what a person is and what he seems to be. This is complicated by the fact that, for different reasons, there may sometimes be no agreement on a person's "real" character. *A fortiori*, opacity may not be too easily detectable. Some people succeed in deceiving others much too easily, while others ("suckers") allow themselves to be deceived time and again. The dynamics of social interaction are too complicated for any simple assumption about "translucency" to hold true. Dissemblance relies not only on one's cunning, but on the *weaknesses* of those with whom one interacts, and the nature of these interactions.

While others have made similar points,[25] perhaps an even more important consideration is this. It is not unrealistic to think that even if someone is a transparent egoist, she may succeed in maximizing her own interests. Rosamond, in *Middlemarch*, is a clear illustration. We shall have occasion to describe her actions in detail in later chapters. The point here is that Rosamond's egoism, though transparent, does not lead to her being shunned. Her behavior, if not explicitly condoned, is at least tolerated. And while the one who suffers most is her husband, Lydgate, he always (gallantly) tries to accommodate her.

Although Rosamond's egoism is confined to securing a rather mindless aristocratic life-style, no one can deny that in the end she maximizes her interests as she conceives of them. In an important sense, Rosamond typifies the conservative social setting of provincial Middlemarch, where birth, rank and class are prominent social boundaries. She, especially, is keenly sensitive to the "aroma of rank" and many of her actions are directed toward association with the aristocracy. In a passage describing Rosamond's accomplished social graces, we are told:

> She was not in the habit of devising falsehoods, and if her statements were no direct clue to the fact, why, they were not intended in that light—they were among her elegant accomplishments, intended to please. Nature had inspired many arts in finishing Mrs. Lemon's favourite pupil, who by general consent...was a rare compound of beauty, cleverness, and amiability. (MM 301).

Rosamond's accomplishments, approved of by her society as part of a cultivated life, have at the same time been a deeply formative aspect of her egoistic character. The social niceties which she has imbibed are a means toward achieving her aims. Her manipulation of Lydgate trades on these niceties. But although she plainly deceives him, this is *not* the deception of *pretending* to accept certain social arrangements while actually holding some other private or personal guide. On the contrary, she acts wholly *within* these arrangements in a way which is legitimized by her society. If morality is seen in contractualist terms as a co-operative venture, Rosamond does not stand outside of such a venture. Instead, she maximizes personal utility both within, and through, such a co-operative matrix.[26]

# Notes

1 These are features which derive from the prescriptivism of R.M. Hare, op. cit. The following debate largely takes his theory as the background of discussion.

2 Hare, *Freedom and Reason*, p. 109.

3 Ibid., chapter 2.

4 George Carlson, "Ethical Egoism Reconsidered," *American Philosophical Quarterly* 10 (1973), p. 25.

5 Brian Medlin, "Ultimate Principles and Ethical Egoism," *Australasian Journal of Philosophy* 35 (1957), p. 114. This paper is reprinted in *Morality and Rational Self-Interest*, edited by D.P. Gauthier (Englewood Cliffs, N.J.: Prentice-Hall, 1970).

6 Jesse Kalin, "In Defense of Egoism," in Gauthier (ed.), op. cit., pp. 73-74.

7 Carlson, op.cit., p. 28.

8 J.A. Brunton, "The Devil Is Not A Fool or Egoism Re-Visited," *American Philosophical Quarterly* 12 (1975).

9 Ibid., p. 324.

10 Ibid., p. 325.

11 *Freedom and Reason*, chapter 9.

12 Ibid., pp. 161, 171 and 173.

13 Hare, *Moral Thinking*, pp. 181-182. Hare discusses fanaticism in terms of the "intuitionistic" attitudes of certain people, who refuse to modify or abandon their moral convictions, e.g. the doctor who refuses to consider ending the life of a suffering, terminally ill patient. Hare argues as if the doctor is weighing the case in terms of his and his colleagues' not preferring to cause themselves the distress of abandoning their moral conviction, against the suffering of the patient. Part of his reply to the objection that this misdescribes the

doctor's reasons is that "moral convictions at the intuitive level are *not* overriding." See p. 178.

14 See Colin Davies, "Egoism and Consistency," *Australasian Journal of Philosophy* 53 (1975), p. 21: "...he must will that others act on their belief. But this does not mean that he must will that he be harmed...." See also Bernard Williams, "Egoism and Altruism," in *Problems of the Self* (Cambridge: Cambridge University Press, 1973). Certain remarks of Thomas Hobbes' are also relevant here: "If the sovereign command a man, though justly condemned, to kill, wound, or maim himself; or not to resist those that assault him; or to abstain from the use of food, air, medicine, or any other thing, without which he cannot live; yet hath that man the liberty to disobey." *Leviathan*, edited by Michael Oakeshott (Oxford: Basil Blackwell, 1955), p. 142 (Part 2 chapter 21).

15 Hare, *Moral Thinking*, pp. 182-183.

16 J.A. Brunton, "Egoism and Morality," *The Philosophical Quarterly* 6 (1956).

17 Brunton, "The Devil is Not a Fool or Egoism Re-Visited," op.cit., p. 329.

18 Ibid.

19 Ibid., pp. 329-330.

20 The locus classicus for contractualism is Hobbes, *Leviathan*, op. cit. An earlier statement can also be found in Plato, *Republic*, op. cit., Book II. More recent articulations have been by Kurt Baier, *The Moral Point of View* (Ithaca, New York: Cornell University Press, 1965), John Rawls, *A Theory of Justice* (Oxford: Oxford University Press, 1972), and most recently, David Gauthier, *Morals by Agreement* (Oxford: Clarendon Press, 1986).

21 Hobbes, op.cit., p. 82 (Part 1 chapter 13).

22 Baier, op. cit, p. 141.

23  See Gauthier, *Morals by Agreement*, op.cit., chapter 6.

24  Ibid., pp. 173-189.

25  See for example, Geoffrey Sayre-McCord, "Deception and Reasons to be Moral," *American Philosophical Quarterly*, 26 (1989).

26  Contractualists will argue that my example of Rosamond is a *non-sequitur*, showing a radical misunderstanding of the contractualist project. John Rawls' technical devices of the original position and the veil of ignorance, for instance, highlight the hypothetical conditions of fairness under which the principles of justice can be chosen. Recent critiques have however shown that this problematically assumes a metaphysical conception of a criterionless self. Similarly, I would argue, Rosamond's identity is not, as such, criterionless but defined by the community of Middlemarch. Her choices, relationships and the possibilities of deception are framed by a particular social milieu. See Rawls, op. cit., and the critiques of Michael J. Sandel, *Liberalism and the Limits of Justice* (Cambridge: Cambridge University Press, 1982), and Alasdair MacIntyre, *After Virtue* (Notre Dame, Indiana: University of Notre Dame Press, 1984).

# Chapter Four

# A Satisfying Morality:
# Desires and Reason for Action

The last two chapters evaluated the coherence of egoism as a moral *principle*. This chapter evaluates its status as a moral *theory*. A principle serves a normative function in making a judgment about the conditions under which one ought to act. While someone may hold a principle as a guide to action, he may not have a moral theory which offers a coherent account and justification of the principle. The key term in ethical egoism is "self-interest." As a principle, ethical egoism advocates the pursuit of self-interest. As a theory, ethical egoism attempts to justify this through an understanding of rationality and self-interest.

Thus the principle of egoism may be supported by two theories of rational action, that (1) only a person's own wants and desires provide him with reasons for acting, and (2) the rational act is that which maximizes the agent's utility. These also offer the possibility that an egoist may have relationships evincing a genuine and direct concern for others. It is held that the egoist—indeed, any (fully) rational agent—would maximize his interests by having such relationships.

I argue that (1) rests on a confusion between being motivated to act and having a reason to act, while (2) distorts the nature of genuine concern. This leads to a discussion of whether the egoist can logically have personal relationships which allow him to maximize self-interest or utility.

The concept of desires is central to this whole discussion. Contemporary moral philosophers, including those not supportive of egoism, have tended to talk of desires without differentiating them. I conclude by emphasizing the non-homogeneity of desires, drawing attention to the concept of a perspective.

## Desires and Reason for Action

One supporter of ethical egoism is Jesse Kalin[1] who proposes the principle:

I    A person ought, all things considered, to do an action if and only if that action is in his overall self-interest.

This is backed by a claim about reason for action:

I′    Only a person's own wants and desires give him reasons for acting.

If I′ is established, so is I, "since a person's self-interest consists in those wants and desires most important to him as determined by his own informed preferential valuation." (Kalin 329). The egoist may, for instance, care about the welfare of another, but "it is only because that other has some special connection with his wants and desires, such as being loved. Only in virtue of this connection can another's wants and desires provide reasons for acting according to I and I′." (Kalin 329).

Both principles appear plausible by contrast with the principle of equal consideration, and its support:

II    A person ought, all things considered, to do an action if and only if that action is in the general interest (where each person's welfare and interests are co-ordinate with every other person's welfare and interests, and each person is regarded as an "end in himself").

II′   Both a person's own wants and desires as well as the wants and desires of others give him reasons for acting.

II′ is interpreted as the claim that "others' wants and desires, and hence their interests, provide reasons irrespective of any connection with the agent's own wants and desires, and hence provide reasons to any and everyone in a position to act upon them." (Kalin 329-330). Kalin argues that we are surer of I′ than II′, for it would be more intelligible to suppose that one's own desires provide one with reasons to act, rather than another's doing so. (For convenience, I shall drop the use of "wants.") Thus, one can abandon the supposition that another's desires provide one with reasons to act without undercutting practical reasoning, since one's own desires remain for consideration. Kalin's reply to the objection that one could just as easily suppose that others' desires provide one with reasons to act whereas one's own do not, is that:

In that case practical reasoning becomes very odd if not unintelligible, for how can M's desire for food for M give N a reason to get food for M and yet not also give M a reason to get food for M? This makes no sense whereas the earlier assumption, that M's desire gave M a reason but did not give N a reason does, for in this case M's wants have a connection to M they do not have to N, namely, the fact that they are *his*. (Kalin 330).

Kalin fails to consider the possibility that "having a desire" is sometimes shorthand for a reason, giving rise to a desire. Such desires are unlike unmotivated ones (e.g. a craving for food), but motivated by certain reasons.[2] In any case, his argument merely stresses (in the above example) that M's desire is M's and not N's. M therefore has reason to satisfy his desire (since it is *his*), whereas it "makes no sense" to suppose, contrariwise, that N has reason to satisfy M's desire.

But Kalin is mistaken. There is a difference between the desire *for* food (hunger) and the desire to *get* food. No doubt N cannot have M's hunger. But M's hunger may quite intelligibly give N a desire (or reason) to get food for M. Moreover, N can have this desire, while M himself may not, despite his hunger.

Kalin could still maintain that N has reason to act only because of a desire for M's welfare, and such a desire can only arise because M's welfare is "somehow" tied to his. This is unsupported, but the relevant point is that Kalin assumes no distinction between reason and desire, whereas his remarks merely show (dubiously) that one has a motivation, only if one has a desire.

Two claims of Kalin's need distinguishing. One is the claim that only one's desires provide reasons for action. The other (an implicit claim) is that only considerations of self-interest (glossed over as a person's "wants and desires most important to him as determined by his own informed preferential valuation") provide reasons for action. Although the first claim could be refuted by making a distinction between prudential reasons and desires,[3] it might be thought that all reasons for action must ultimately rest on considerations of self-interest (the second claim). However, it is precisely this which needs argument, which Kalin fails to provide. In any case, since the argument for I' is invalid, there is no support for I, the principle of egoism.

### Desires and Rational (Informed) Action

Richard Brandt[4] provides the missing argument by defining "rational action" such that it necessarily encompasses self-interested action. For Brandt, an act is "rational" for a certain person at a certain time when it is:

> the action that person *actually would* perform at that time if (a) his desires and aversions at the time were what they would be if he had been fully exposed to available information, and if (b) the agent had firmly and vividly in mind, and equally at the center of attention, all those knowable facts which, if he thought about them, would make a difference to his tendency to act, given his "cleaned-up" desires [as in (a)]. (Brandt 682).

Brandt adds that he is using "rational" action to essentially mean "fully informed" action. This definition is advanced as an interpretation of a necessary condition of ethical egoism, viz., "the rational act is that which maximizes the agent's long-range (expectable) utility." This is true provided (1) "utility" is defined "in terms of the intensity of his desire, at the time, for various outcomes, or features of the act itself" and (2) as indicated above, his desires have been "cleaned-up."[5]

Although (2) suggests that desires are not uncriticizable, it nonetheless transpires that (through the definition of "utility," and the acceptance of the necessary condition mentioned) the concern of a rational agent is primarily the maximal satisfaction of his desires.

The term "desire," used interchangeably with "want," is however, broadly construed:

> ...my act may be perfectly rational (or well-informed) if it sacrifices some personal pleasure for the happiness or security of my daughter, or for the discomfort of my chairman, or doubtless, for all sorts of causes or ideals, provided I really do want these things. Thus it is just not true that it is rational for me to sacrifice a personal enjoyment *only* for the sake of some desired state of my person in the narrow sense—such as eating a good meal, having sex, or glowing from admiration. I find nothing surprising in this. If I really care about my daughter's welfare, why is it not rational for me to sacrifice some personal pleasure to that end? (Brandt 685).

The above examples are distinguished in terms of "external" and "internal" desires (e.g. his daughter's welfare and a good meal, respectively). This enables Brandt to claim, against the narrow internal construal of "desires," that an egoist may legitimately be described as desiring another's welfare.

But perhaps the persuasiveness of this account is enhanced by the following implicit contrasts.[6] I may seek another's welfare because:

(a)  I am (genuinely) concerned about his welfare.
(b)  I feel that I have an obligation.
(c)  It is part of the job (say, as a welfare officer).

Assuming for the sake of argument that these are mutually exclusive, (b) would not be described as desiring another's welfare (we can strengthen this by assuming that I do not care for the person but nonetheless acknowledge a duty), and (c) could be described, more accurately, as desiring to do my job well.  By contrast, Brandt's terminology of seeking to satisfy a desire for another's welfare seems to be a perfect description of (a), where, *ex hypothesi*, there is genuine concern.

Two issues arise.  First, whether the description of genuine concern as seeking to satisfy a desire is accurate.  Second, whether the conscious and consistent aim for utility maximization is compatible with genuine concern.  This second issue is important because of the assumption that the egoist's utility would be maximized if he formed personal relationships, the basis of which calls for care and concern.  I shall take up the first issue shortly, while the second issue will be discussed in the next section.

Before going further, it is best to be clear about what Brandt implicitly holds as a reason for action.  The following remarks indicate that his distinction between "external" or "benevolent" desires on the one hand, and "internal" ones on the other, is spurious:

> ...I hold that if I really desire the happiness of my daughter, or the discomfiture of my department chairman, or some cause or ideal, then *getting that desire satisfied*—i.e., the occurrence of the event or state of affairs desired—counts as being an enhancement of my utility or welfare...and counts to an extent corresponding to how strongly I want that outcome. (Brandt 686, italics mine).

For Brandt, what *counts* is not so much that the (external) state of affairs desired be realized—though this is important as a means—but rather, the enhancement of the agent's utility, defined as we have seen, in terms of the maximal satisfaction of his (cleaned-up) desires.[7]

The claim that an act is irrational if it does not maximize utility is doubtful. One may have reasons to act other than utility maximization. This raises the question whether actions expressing concern for others are, at the same time, utility maximizing.

Consider this example. X has a responsible colleague, Y. Recently however, Y has been turning up late, performing his duties mechanically, looking extremely tired and sad. He is not inconveniencing anyone but after a couple of days, X becomes concerned about him. Despite the fact that his wife is ill and expects him home early to do the chores and mind the kids, he decides that he really must talk to Y. He telephones home, has a hard time explaining things to his wife, and takes Y out for a drink. Y gets drunk and pours out his sorrows. X tries his best to comfort Y, though knowing he cannot help. After several hours, X suggests that Y had better go home. He has difficulties escorting Y home, losing his wallet in the process. The next morning, he is late for an important appointment.

X cannot be said to be maximizing utility because the actions expressing his concern involve events which he could not be said to desire. Neither is he minimizing utility, however. Although X may have sacrificed his own time and projects, he need not see it like this. It is one indication of his concern for Y that he does not see it as a sacrifice. Suppose his wife mentions that she fails to understand his "sacrifice" for Y. There is no indication that X has made a sacrifice if he replies, "You don't understand. You should have seen the state he was in. He's had this problem for years now, and it has all suddenly erupted. The poor man just needed someone to talk to. There's nothing I can do to help really (i.e. you don't have to worry about my having to make further 'sacrifices'), I just hope for his sake that things will brighten up soon."

X would more appropriately think of his actions as a sacrifice if they were motivated by something other than a concern for Y. For instance, if Y were his superior who would be more kindly disposed toward him later, perhaps enhancing his chances of a promotion. Or if X for some reason later comes to regret his actions, he may then see them as involving a sacrifice. But assuming that there is neither such motivation nor regret, the reason for X's actions is not that he wanted to maximize personal utility, but simply that he was concerned about Y.

It may be replied that in as much as X desired Y's welfare, he has maximized his utility in satisfying that desire. However, this will not work. If an act is aimed at maximizing utility, then it is criticizable on the ground that it was inefficient. Such a criticism is inapplicable to X's actions. In order to see this, contrast the following cases:

(1) A group of soldiers desire to reach a point, P. After overcoming tremendous obstacles, they happily arrive at P. But instead of being commended, they are castigated for not discovering a less obstructive route.

(2) A, knowing that her friend, B, is deeply depressed, goes to great lengths to prevent B from hearing a piece of bad news, waiting until B would be emotionally prepared before breaking it to her. Another friend, Z, equally concerned, nonetheless thinks that some of the things A does are quite unnecessary. Although these are designed to protect B, he thinks they are unlikely to help in any way. In general, Z thinks that A is muddled and "making too much of a fuss."

Although there are limits to what A may do without being criticized as inefficient, nonetheless, A may not be similarly criticized as the soldiers. Her "making too much of a fuss" is commendable, as it shows concern. On the other hand, if the soldiers were described as having been overly fussy (i.e. wasted too much time and energy) in the execution of their plans, this could in no way be commendable. Although A's concern may be described as a desire for B's welfare, it is B's welfare she is concerned about, and the failure to act efficiently is not, within limits, what is important here. (This does not deny that there are occasions where, in helping someone, efficiency is of the utmost importance.)

Further, if there is no way of promoting another's welfare, one's concern—described as seeking to satisfy a desire—seems hopelessly futile. Such a desire would have nothing to get its grip on, it would be left unfulfilled, and it would have no cash value. The concern for another is not similarly placed. Our earlier example showed that even though there may be no way in which X can promote Y's welfare, X may still be said to be concerned about Y.

My arguments may be consolidated by examining the following example:

Dorothea...felt some disappointment...that there was nothing for her to do in Lowick; and in the next few minutes her mind had glanced over the possibility, which she would have preferred, of finding that her home would be in a parish which had a larger share of the world's misery, so that she might have had more active duties in it. (MM 103).

Dorothea's desire to improve the welfare of the villagers is motivated by another, that it is *she* who betters their welfare. That is, she is highly conscious of being someone who is good, and very much desires that she be such a person.[8] It may be true to describe Dorothea as getting a desire satisfied, when she acts to secure the welfare of others. But in the absence of such a context, the locution of "satisfying a desire" that another's welfare be bettered is but a cumbersome and misleading way of saying that another's welfare *is* bettered.[9]

Suppose this last point is denied and it is asserted that there are two items here, (1) occurrence of the object (welfare improvement) and (2) satisfaction of the (benevolent) desire. It is the desire which motivationally explains the action leading to the occurrence of the object. The claim that (1) and (2) are equivalent leaves out the necessary motivational consideration.[10]

However, it would still not follow that satisfying a desire is essential to concern. As we have seen, the nature of concern is such that one may still be concerned (indeed, even more so) where there is no possibility of improving the other's welfare. This is not analogous, say, to someone's having a futile desire to own a piece of property. In this case, he would do better to look for a substitute. The point is not so much that it would be irrational of him to continue desiring this particular property (it is not irrational if the property has unique qualities), rather than that it is logically possible for him to direct his desire elsewhere.[11]

If we look at concern in terms of this model of desire, however, we could not understand it. For then it would indeed be irrational if one continues to desire another's welfare, while knowing full well it cannot be satisfied. But it is precisely this "irrationality" that is characteristic of (genuine) concern. In contrast to the example of desiring a piece of property, we may say that concern cannot be re-directed or transferred.[12] My desire for X's welfare is a desire for *X's* welfare. It would be absurd to think, since circumstances do not permit me to satisfy this desire, that I should therefore transfer it. Or if not absurd, then (perhaps like Dorothea) this may not be a case of genuine concern—finding no opportunity here to exercise my charity, I go elsewhere.

## Friendship

Jesse Kalin has suggested the possibility of the egoist's "establishing enduring relationships of friendship and love."[13]   As this is never fully spelled out, let us try and construct  what the egoistic conception of friendship amounts to.

Thus, it may be said that it is in one's overall interest to have friends. One's friends are, in a sense, an extension of oneself—what promotes their interests simultaneously promotes one's own.[14] It is undeniable that one gets certain "goods" and "benefits" out of friendship, e.g. the joys and pleasures of companionship; the emotions of warmth, intimacy, and security in having someone to rely on and trust; a comforting sense of belonging, having a sense of one's worth, of being wanted, these being affirmed by the trust and confidence which others have in one; relatedly, having a sense of well-being which comes out of the affection others have for one; and reciprocally, there is also the happiness of knowing that someone whom one likes is flourishing.  On the egoistic perspective, since it is one's conscious aim as a fully rational being to maximize self-interest, it is *for the sake of* these "goods" and "benefits" that one enters into friendship.  It is for this reason that one identifies with another, a "friend."

If these "goods" and "benefits" were absent then there would be no friendship to speak of.  But contrary to the egoistic conception, it does not follow that it is "for the sake of" these things that a friendship comes about.  Consider in this connection, the kind of identification which the character Mrs. Bulstrode has with her husband, as described in *Middlemarch*.  Mr. Bulstrode is facing disgrace and bracing himself to meet his wife:

> He raised his eyes with a little start and looked at her half amazed for a moment:  her pale face, her changed, mourning dress, the trembling about her mouth, all said, 'I know'; and her hands and eyes rested gently on him...They could not yet speak to each other of the shame which she was bearing with him, or of the acts which had brought it down on them.  His confession was silent, and her promise of faithfulness was silent.  Open-minded as she was, she nevertheless shrank from the words which would have expressed their mutual consciousness, as she would have shrunk from flakes of fire.  She could not say, 'How much is only slander and false suspicion?' and he did not say, 'I am innocent.' (MM 807-08).

Mrs. Bulstrode does not identify herself with her husband in the sense that she desires the "goods" and "benefits" described earlier. Instead, to say that she identifies with him is to say that she cares and is concerned for *him*. And the extent to which she is able to identify herself with him —which is not the same as identifying her interests with his, though of course, their interests are not unrelated—is an indication of the degree to which she cares for him. The emotions and feelings which they are able to express privately, their sharing of a silent communication are not, absurdly, things "for the sake of which" they aimed at in establishing a relationship. Rather, these have been nurtured out of their mutual care and concern.

None of this rules out the possibility that someone may enter into a relationship with the express aim of gaining something. The point remains, however, that unless there is or comes to be care and concern, there can be no close personal relationship to speak of. This point is relevant to the ethical egoist. If he expresses care and concern in the ways described above, then he can no longer be said to be consciously aiming at maximizing self-interest.

But suppose it were argued that it is not unintelligible to think of the egoist as having an affection for someone, while conscious of the aim of maximizing self-interest. Why should they be incompatible? My reply is that much depends on the degree of affection and the nature of the friendship. So far, we have not distinguished among different kinds of friendship.[15] Thus, not all kinds of friendship are ruled out for the egoist. One may have a friend whose company one enjoys, but for whom one cares little or not at all, and some friends are those whose companionship it would be advantageous or pleasurable to have. An egoist is not precluded from these friendships. The suggestion that the egoist is capable of gaining fully the benefits of friendship, however, means to assert that he is capable of going beyond friendships of these sorts.

One source of the egoistic conception of friendship rests, finally, on the idea that friendship is not an impartial or a disinterested phenomenon. This may, misleadingly, lead one to think that friendship is an egoistic phenomenon. If this implies that in doing something for a friend, one at the same time helps oneself, then we have already analyzed the mistake as lying in the ambiguity of "identifying" oneself with one's friend, i.e. either caring for another, or merely having a stake in his interests.

On the other hand, a clash might sometimes exist between acting for a friend or a stranger. But if I act in favour of my friend, this is not necessarily inappropriate or egoistic. How my action is to be interpreted

depends on the circumstances. It is egoistic if I act for my friend at
another's expense. However, this is not because I am doing something
for my friend *per se*, but because I am ignoring the justifiable claims of
another.

Nevertheless, there are other occasions in which it would not be
unjustified or inappropriate to act for (or in favour of) my friend.[16] Also,
not everything that I can do for my friend may be appropriate for others.
My friend can confide in me, I can give him emotional support, admonish
or advise him (in ways which, applied to others, may be offensive), I can
cheer him up simply by being with him, we can make "silent
confessions," etc. These are not manifestations of egoism. Rather, they
are indications of the possibility of the deepest care and concern which
one human being can have for another.

## Desires and Perspectives

Recently, philosophers reacting against the Kantian focus on duty and
the impersonal considerations of utilitarianism (or consequentialism) have
also emphasized the role of desires as providing reasons for action.
These positions are manifestly non-egoistic and give room for a variety
of desires other than self-interest. They refer to commitments to various
projects and personal ideals which may override the imposition of an
impersonal morality.[17] Although allowing a rightful place for the
emotions and spontaneity within morality, the weakness of these Humean
positions is that they fail to differentiate the natures of the various desires.
As such, they also fail to counter the impression of a "high-minded"
egoism.

To go beyond this, it is important to see how desires may allow us to
talk of perspectives. A particular perspective is defined by the nature of
the desire involved. The following example, borrowed from Derek
Parfit,[18] illustrates this quite well. Kate, a writer, desires her books to be
as good as possible. But because she works so hard, she collapses with
exhaustion and is, for a period, very depressed. Although Kate believes
that if she worked less hard, she would be happier, she would only be
doing so if she had a weaker desire that her books be as good as possible.
Further, although in self-interested terms, Kate is doing what is worse for
herself, and hence acting irrationally, *she* is not irrational. She could
work less hard, but this would come about only if her desire to make her
books as good as possible were weaker. This would however, be on the
whole, worse for her—she would find her work boring. Thus, although

she knowingly does what she believes to be irrational, she is not acting irrationally.

Parfit is here arguing against the claim of irrationality, or more specifically, self-defeatingness regarding certain self-interested policies. We may take the example, however, to illustrate a "perspective." Thus, the fact that Kate desires her books to be as good as possible, even if her health suffers, is to be described in terms of what she "sees" in her activity. Her reason for action therefore, is not simply that she *desires* that her books be as good as possible, but that what she does, seen in terms internal to her work, is meaningful. The description of what is meaningful here is the perspective which makes her absorbed in her work.[19]

Parfit himself (although not a Humean in the sense described above but a utilitarian), while arguing that desires are inherently criticizable, is unable to get away from the primacy of desires. He argues that certain desires may be intrinsically irrational, e.g. desires which demonstrate a temporal and positional arbitrariness, such as caring less for a future pain because it will be more than a year away, and caring less about the suffering of others because they are more than a mile away.[20] Other desires, on the other hand, may be rationally required, e.g. to care about morality, and to care about the needs of others. In these cases, we have reason to act morally, even if we have no desire to do so.[21]

The trouble, however, is that Parfit leaves open the validity of the last claim and in fact finds it difficult to justify. As he says, "on the moral theories that most of us accept, morality does not provide the only reasons for acting. On these theories, there are many cases where we could act in several different ways, and none of these acts would be morally better than the others. In these cases, even if we accept CPM,[22] what we have most reason to do will depend in part on what our present desires are."[23] Thus, while trying to place an emphasis on reason for action, and the idea of what is worth desiring, Parfit is yet, as stated earlier, unable to get away from the primacy of desire.

Further evidence of this lies in the way he handles an example like the "heroic death." Similar to the example of Kate, this is narrowly construed in terms of what the agent "desires." His description goes like this:

I choose to die in a way that I know will be painful, but will save the lives of several other people. I am doing what, knowing the facts and thinking clearly, I most want to do, and what best fulfils my present desires. (In all my examples these two coincide.) I also know that I am doing what will be worse for me. If I did not sacrifice my life, to save these other people, I would not be haunted by remorse. The rest of my life would be well worth living.[24]

Although Parfit does go on to talk of caring more about the survival of others than about one's own survival, it is unclear that if one talks of "choice" and "fulfilling one's desires" here, that one has captured the notion of "worth" that he was initially after. Thus, a more sensitive account of the case may reveal that the person saw only one thing he "must" do, i.e. save the lives of others (even if it means his own painful death). He did not, in other words, see a choice here.[25] The reason for his action is specified, perhaps (though not necessarily consciously), in the following terms: "The others will surely die if I don't do something, I know that this means my own painful death, but I must do something." This is not a reason which he can "justify" to others, nor need it be articulated—in this sense, it is not a "reason for action," so much as a perspective from which the action is carried out. Justification assumes a context in which the reason one gives is challengeable, or where there is a need to convince others—perhaps to do the same (kind of) action. However, the "I must" or "I have no alternative" in the kind of case under consideration, does not imply that others too must do the same.

Where the notion of a choice for the agent is inoperative here, so too is the notion of "desire"—to care about the lives of others to the extent that one is willing to die to ensure their survival cannot merely be described as "desiring" or "preferring" their survival. Some tyrant may do the same, i.e. he may "desire" the survival of some, and he may "prefer" it. And if he were a mad tyrant, he may have this desire or preference that they live, and he die—perhaps to show that there is something ultimate in what *he* desires, prefers, or wills.

# Notes

1 Jesse Kalin, "Two Kinds of Moral Reasoning: Ethical Egoism As A Moral Theory," *Canadian Journal of Philosophy* 5 (1975).

2 See Thomas Nagel, *The Possibility of Altruism* (Oxford: Oxford University Press, 1970), pp. 29-30.

3 See for instance, the discussion by G.R. Grice, *The Grounds of Moral Judgment* (Cambridge: Cambridge University Press, 1967), chapter 1.

4 Richard Brandt, "Rationality, Egoism and Morality," *The Journal of Philosophy* 69 (1972).

5 Brandt is referring to the purported fact that certain desires or aversions that some people might have, e.g., an intense craving for recognition, or an aversion to being in a certain occupation, would disappear if such people were to be "fully exposed to available information," or rather, as he says, "if they repeatedly brought to mind, with full belief and maximal vividness, all the knowable facts that would tend either to weaken or to strengthen the desire or aversion, or, as we might say, if the person were to go through 'cognitive psychotherapy'." This is developed further in his book, *A Theory of the Good and the Right* (Oxford: Clarendon Press, 1979). See my discussion in chapter 6.

6 I thank Robert Stecker for suggesting this point.

7 A related difficulty for Brandt's account has been noted by Mark Overvold and Brandt himself. Thus, for instance, an act of self-sacrifice may be the object of an informed desire, and when fulfilled, increases the agent's welfare. Self-sacrifice thus becomes self-interest. See Overvold, "Self-Interest and the Concept of Self-Sacrifice," *Canadian Journal of Philosophy* 10 (1980); "Self-Interest and Getting What You Want," in *The Limits of Utilitarianism*, edited by H.B. Miller & W.H. Williams (Minneapolis: University of Minnesota Press, 1982); and Brandt, "Two Concepts of Utility," in H.B. Miller & W.H. Williams, op. cit.

8 Although I am using the example to illustrate using others to satisfy a desire (for moral perfection), it is unclear that the example need be

interpreted like this. Thus, Dorothea could be said to be having a conception of herself as a person of a certain sort, and trying to live up to this image of herself. This is what Harry Frankfurt refers to as a "second-order" desire which helps to define a person. See H.G. Frankfurt, "Freedom of the Will and the Concept of a Person," *Journal of Philosophy* 68 (1971).

9 The fact that desire is externally directed at an object, and that there could be various objects other than self-interest was forcefully argued by Bishop Joseph Butler. See especially the "Preface" and "Sermon XI" of *Butler's Sermons* edited by Rev. W.R. Matthews (London: G. Bell and Sons Ltd., 1969).

10 One common feature of major psychological theories of the past century (from Freud, Skinner, to contemporary sociobiologists like Wilson and Dawkins) has been an emphasis on the essentially self-centered basis of human motivation, including moral and generally altruistic behavior. Thus, the sociobiologists have analyzed altruistic behaviour in animals and man as no more and no less than simply the outcome of "evolutionary stable strategies" for the propagation of the individual's genetic material. See E.O. Wilson, *Sociobiology: The New Synthesis* (Cambridge, Massachusetts: Harvard University Press, 1975) and R. Dawkins, *The Selfish Gene* (Oxford: Oxford University Press, 1976). If correct, my argument about the logic of concern as different from the logic of desires would also apply to these theories. I thank John Greenwood for drawing my attention to these theories. Incidentally, insofar as a discussion of egoism as a moral theory involves the discussion of motivational considerations, the usual textbook distinction between a descriptive "psychological egoism" and a prescriptive "ethical egoism" should no longer hold.

11 While distinguishing between desire and affection and noting the replaceability of the objects of desire, J.L. Stocks describes the principle of desire as "the mere vehicle of a motion which ends in the organism in which it begins." Stocks, *The Limits of Purpose and Other Essays* (London: Ernest Benn Ltd. 1932), p. 39. See also the volume of Stocks' work edited and with an introduction by D.Z. Phillips, *Morality and Purpose* (London: Routledge and Kegan Paul, 1969).

12 A distinction between transferable and non-transferable attitudes has also been made by Roger Scruton, *Sexual Desire* (London: Weidenfeld and Nicolson, 1986), p. 103. To anticipate a possible criticism, it is possible that just as one may lose a desire to acquire a piece of property, so too, may one cease to feel concern for another. However, this possibility does not affect the point about the non-transferability of concern, and we should also not assume that the circumstances surrounding the loss of desire and ceasing to feel concern are of the same explanatory order.

13 Kalin, op. cit., p. 335. It is not important for my purpose to distinguish between love and friendship, and for simplicity's sake, I shall henceforth only use the term, "friendship."

14 Lawrence Blum, *Friendship, Altruism and Morality* (London: Routledge and Kegan Paul, 1980). See especially pp. 75-77. I owe to him detection of the ambiguity of what it means to "identify" oneself with another (see the discussion below).

15 Aristotle distinguishes three kinds of friendship, based on utility, pleasure, and goodness. The third represents perfect friendship: "... friendship in the primary and proper sense is between good men in virtue of their goodness, whereas the rest are friendships only by analogy." *Nicomachean Ethics* Book 8 1157a10-34. Aristotle would distinguish affection from this conception of perfect friendship, because affection "resembles a feeling," but friendship is a (moral) state. "For affection can be felt equally well for inanimate objects, but mutual affection involves choice, and choice proceeds from a (moral) state." 1157b21-1158a7. The above translations are by J.A.K. Thomson, *The Ethics of Aristotle: The Nicomachean Ethics* (Harmondsworth: Penguin, 1976), p. 265 and p. 267.

16 See chapter 3 of Blum, *Friendship, Altruism and Morality*, for an excellent discussion of this.

17 See Bernard Williams, "Internal and External Reasons" and "Moral Luck," both in *Moral Luck*, and *Ethics and the Limits of Philosophy*, especially chapter 10, "Morality, the Peculiar Institution." (All references given in note 12 of chapter 1. Note my qualification of Williams' position there and in note 21 of chapter 6.) Also Philippa

Foot, "Morality as a System of Hypothetical Imperatives," in *Virtues and Vices* (see note 12, chapter 1) and Susan Wolf, "Moral Saints," *Journal of Philosophy* 79 (1982).

18 Derek Parfit, *Reasons and Persons* (Oxford: Oxford University Press, 1984), pp. 6-9 and pp. 14-16.

19 See Michael Weston, *Morality and the Self*, (Oxford: Basil Blackwell, 1975), chapter 2, for examples of the way in which a man's relation to a goal may be described internally, in terms of "what he sees" in the activity which he is pursuing.

20 Parfit, op.cit., pp. 123-126.

21 Ibid., pp. 121-122.

22 "CPM" refers to a version of what Parfit calls the "critical present-aim" theory. CPM states that "each of us is rationally required to care about morality, and this desire is supremely rational. It is irrational to care as much about anything else."

23 Ibid., p. 133.

24 Ibid., p. 132.

25 For example, see Michael Weston's (note 19 above) discussion of Conrad's *Lord Jim*. Bernard Williams also discusses the notion of a "must", or a "necessity", in non-Kantian terms, in *Shame and Necessity* (Berkeley: University of California Press, 1993), especially chapter 4, "Shame and Autonomy."

# Chapter Five

## Personal and Impersonal

The failure of egoism as a theory explaining moral phenomena does not detract from its rationality. However, it is the rational attitude underlying egoism which offends moral sensibilities. Reference has been made in previous chapters to the examples of Rosamond and Dorothea, from *Middlemarch*. This chapter narrates and contrasts the two. While allowing those unfamiliar with the novel a better grasp of the examples, the narratives also diagnose the failure to both convict egoism of irrationality and to ground morality rationally.

The narratives focus on two entirely different senses of a "problem." Rosamond illustrates a means-end rationality. The sense in which Dorothea has a "problem" facing her, in the situation to be described, is less straightforward. Through her concern for her husband Casaubon, Dorothea gets into a quandary. This indicates that it is she herself who generates the "problem." In other words, she has a moral perspective which is personal.

Dorothea's concern is expressed in a way which does not presuppose the judgment that "Anyone ought to do the same, under relevantly similar circumstances." The possibility of such a judgment depends on there being a reason or reasons for acting, which can be translated into universal or impersonal terms. There are at least three contexts where impersonal reasons may usually apply.

One is where someone wishes to evade her duty by making an exception of herself. To ask her for the principle underlying her action, that anyone ought to do the same, suggests that she ought not make an exception of herself and this is a *moral* criticism. It has already been argued however (in chapter 3), that one who is clear about what she is doing, and prepared to accept the consequences of her action while extending the underlying principle to others, cannot be accused of inconsistency. She is, in the logical sense required, acting on impersonal grounds.

In the second, institutional context, anyone in a certain position is expected to perform a certain role and to act on certain standards. As was earlier shown, there are (moral) cases where some expectations may be challenged. It was also argued that the egoist can work within an institutional or contractual framework (see chapters 2 and 3).

Substitute Rosamond for the egoist in the earlier chapters, and it may be seen how she could fulfil the criteria of rationality said to govern these two contexts. However, the means-end complex more directly characterizes her. Anyone who wills the end also wills the relevant and most appropriate means. Whether one has made a mistake, in this context, is ascertainable by the standards set by the end. This is a third context therefore, where we may make sense of the universal injunction, "Anyone ought to do the same, under relevantly similar circumstances." In this regard, the following contrast will show how impersonal or universal reasons may be said to underlie the egoism of Rosamond but not the concern evinced by Dorothea. This would constitute the diagnosis referred to above.

## Rosamond

Rosamond's actions are dominated by the end of attaining social rank. She behaves faultlessly, as expected of a young lady from a middle-class family. At the same time, this propriety goes beyond a convenient observance of etiquette. She is, for instance, indignant about her brother's dereliction of duty in not wanting to become a clergyman. To her, it does not matter that he is temperamentally unfit for this role, for within the socially arranged scheme of things, he *ought* to take it up. This is not some kind of "corrupt" morality that Rosamond is manifesting, but a common part of moral life—the expectations and fulfilment of roles and responsibilities. At the same time this sense of propriety makes others think well of her, thus helping her social ambitions.

More than anyone else, we might say, Rosamond has a guide to action. The central opportunity which comes her way is Lydgate's introduction to Middlemarch society. Marriage to him opens up vistas of association with noble relatives and in general, an aristocratic lifestyle. Naturally, there are obstacles. For instance, Lydgate's disdain for matters and people associated with rank, his absorbing interest in medicine (which has low social esteem) and a practical attitude in dealing with debts resulting from setting up house in a grand style—the return of furniture, selling the house and living in a smaller one. In short, measures which directly counter Rosamond's concerns. Attempts to overcome these obstacles carry attendant risks, e.g. that Lydgate might not bend to her will, or that she might make a wrong calculation.

The first risk is surmounted by skilful manipulation of Lydgates's gallantry and sense of propriety, i.e. the thought that in marrying him, she had fallen into destitution, and it was up to him to keep her happy. And when her letter to Lydgate's uncle asking for money (giving the impression that it was written at Lydgate's behest) backfires (Lydgate receiving a humiliating reply) Rosamond adopts the attitude—partly out of pride, but also as a calculated means of protecting herself and keeping options open—that she had done her best and is faultless. This attitude has the following effect on Lydgate:

> Lydgate sat paralysed by opposing impulses: since no reasoning he could apply to Rosamond seemed likely to conquer her assent, he wanted to smash and grind some object on which he could produce an impression, or else to tell her brutally that he was master, and she must obey. But he not only dreaded the effect of such extremities on their mutual life—he had a growing dread of Rosamond's quiet elusive obstinacy, which would not allow any assertion of power to be final; and again, she had touched him in a spot of keenest feeling by implying that she had been deluded with a false vision of happiness in marrying him. As to saying he was master, it was not the fact. The very resolution to which he had wrought himself by dint of logic and honourable pride was beginning to relax under her torpedo contact.... (MM 710-711).

We may say, with some justification, that Rosamond's relationship with Lydgate is reduced to that of force, since this explains a crucial aspect of her character, i.e. her incapacity for moral development or change. And this in turn, is due partly to the fact that one can never reason or quarrel with her. This can be explained as follows.

The pressure of force is a double-edged one. The person who is intoxicated by force (Rosamond "welcomed the signs that her husband...was under control") also becomes a thing (while treating another as a thing to be manipulated or forced). Having dropped to the level of force in forging a relationship now categorized by "weak" and "strong," she also becomes inert and impassive.[1]  Rosamond's relationship to (rather than with) Lydgate is one of gradual mastery, through a quiet, elusive and  obstinate force. Her resolute push for the results which she wants means that Lydgate should see things the way she does, and do things the way she wants them, since she does not want anything else.

Reasoning, arguing, and quarreling mean that one subjects oneself to the influence of the other's opinions and emotions, perhaps revealing aspects of both parties to which one may have been blind. The impact of an emotional exchange may result in a change of perspective. This does not mean that the outlook for both will permanently improve but at least the *possibility* of change and development is there.

Rosamond, however, *inures* herself in advance to the impact of the other's opinions and feelings. One cannot (have a) quarrel with her because she never *involves* herself in the quarrel.[2] She does not respond to argument, but is left cold by it. Lydgate may not be said to have a moral relation with her and, as such, she is immune to moral change.

## Dorothea

Dorothea forms a contrast. Her actions, as described in the later chapters of *Middlemarch*, are not carried out from the perspective of a goal which provides her with a guide, but on the contrary, manifest a moral development which takes her *away* from such a perspective.

Her earlier insensitive behavior is indirectly the result of her spiritual quest for perfection. She confusedly links this with intellectual accomplishment, believing that it would at the same time enable her to satisfy a yearning to perform "the good." She marries Casaubon because she thinks (mistakenly) that he represents these spiritual, moral and intellectual ideals. Her confusion about these ideals makes her insensitive however, to everything except what is deemed relevant or worthy to the quest for perfection.

For instance, her sister Celia suggests that they divide between them the jewels left by their late mother. Dorothea adopts a superior tone when she tells Celia that she could have them all, and with a hint of puritanic toleration, "There—take away your property." But a moment later, she is herself attracted by a ring and bracelet (for which Celia had already indicated a liking), and gives them a spiritual association: "All the while her thought was trying to justify her delight in the colours by merging them in her mystic joy." She decides to keep them despite a wavering thought that "Yet what miserable men find such things and work at them, and sell them!" She again insensitively tells her sister to "take the rest away." Celia, wondering whether Dorothea was not being somewhat inconsistent, innocently asks, "Shall you wear them in company?" Dorothea's haughty reply is cutting: "Perhaps...I cannot tell to what level I may sink." (MM 35-36).

But though confused and immature, Dorothea's morally ardent nature is genuine. What this means will come out if we compare the change which revelation of Casaubon's true character eventually brings about in her, with the concept of change within the means-end complex. In the latter, a change in circumstances may make a particular means no longer desirable. Instead, it may now be an obstacle. For instance, when Lydgate becomes tainted through suspicion of his professional integrity, Rosamond wishes she had never met him.

In Dorothea's case, disappointment with Casaubon, though frustrating, does not lead to a similar view. Rather, the revelation of Casaubon's shallowness, together with alarming intimations of the worthlessness of his academic work and the meaninglessness of his life's course which that implies—these new perceptions form the beginning of her moral development. Her earlier confused idea of "doing good," although blended with the goal of intellectual accomplishment, is not abandoned, once the latter is seen to be an illusion, at least as personified in Casaubon. To see this, we need to understand the significance of the new perceptions concerning Casaubon.

Where before, Dorothea saw him as merely relevant and worthy in relation to a goal, quarrel with him and his subsequent illness leads her to realize his weak and sensitive nature. Although the earlier perspective classified him as relevant, it catered to just one side of her mixed motives in marrying him. These were, not only to become learned, but also devotion to a vague conception of "the good." The new perception of Casaubon destroys these intellectual pretensions (although she does learn something here). Nonetheless, a situation arises at the same time, where goodness could be applied.

Her moral development consists in the perception that there were some things to which she had been blind, given her devotion to vague ideals. In particular, she comes to realize that she had been ignorant and indifferent to aspects of a person's character and situation, which indicate as great a need on his side, as on her own. This revelation is all the more striking because it concerns someone whom she had closely relied on. These new perceptions of Casaubon therefore, are significant because they constitute moral modalities. These include the perception that she had been neglecting him; had failed to be aware of his needs, although (and the realization of this is what is terrible) she should have been the person closest to him; that further, she had selfishly only sought to make use of him, and in that respect, shameful to say, taken note only of aspects which are merely relevant to her own concerns; and that he has after all "an equivalent centre of self" which merits attention.

As we have seen, under the means-end complex, obstacles are

so-called because they ought to be removed if the goal is to be achieved. To give a brief illustration: when Lydgate demands a promise from Rosamond not to go horse-riding again (during her pregnancy), Rosamond manipulates this into a promise from *him* not to interfere, thereby removing an obstacle to her plans. Lydgate has just said that he would tell his (stylishly aristocratic) cousin off for taking her riding:

'I beg you will not do anything of the kind, Tertius,' said Rosamond, looking at him with something more marked than usual in her speech. 'It will be treating me as if I were a child. Promise that you will leave the subject to me.'

There did seem to be some truth in her objection. Lydgate said, 'Very well,' with a surly obedience, and thus the discussion ended with his promising Rosamond, and not with her promising him. (MM 630).

Dorothea's perceptions, on the other hand, present her with an "obstacle" which is not defined as something to be removed, but rather, constitutes a moral perspective. That is, they carry a concern for the other person together with certain demands (e.g. that one make amends, be more responsive to the other's needs, be less self-assertive, etc.). Reference to an "obstacle" here implies that one cannot have the perceptions mentioned and remain indifferent. Having them means at the same time, recognizing the corresponding demands.

It might be argued that Casaubon, as George Eliot describes him, does not deserve the kind of response that Dorothea evinces. In the next chapter, I shall examine the tenability and logical status of this claim. For now, suffice it to say that it is *Dorothea* who evinces these responses and though "we" may not agree, it is not unintelligible for her to respond as she does. We may illustrate how the concern shown by Dorothea cannot be said to be based on any universal principle, nor is she committed to holding any such principle. While the concern which she expresses for Casaubon may be called a "reason for acting," this does not imply that it is *grounded* in reason, insofar as "reason" in this latter case involves a universal principle.

There is an interview between Dorothea and Lydgate in which she asks to be told plainly about Casaubon's state of health, following his collapse. She cannot bear to be unaware of something which might have made her act differently (perhaps more gently, toward Casaubon).

Lydgate replies that "it is one's function as a medical man to hinder regrets of that sort as far as possible." He warns against excessive work and mental agitation for Casaubon, advising that all means should be taken to moderate and vary his occupations. Dorothea asks for more specific guidance:

'Help me, pray,' she said, at last, in the same low voice as before. 'Tell me what I can do.' (MM 323).

Lydgate suggests travel but on learning this will not do (Dorothea remembering the friction between Casaubon and herself during their recent sojourn), repeats that Casaubon should not overwork or be made anxious. At the end of the interview, Lydgate rises:

He was bowing and quitting her, when an impulse which if she had been alone would have turned into a prayer, made her say with a sob in her voice—

'Oh, you are a wise man, are you not? You know all about life and death. Advise me. Think what I can do. He has been labouring all his life and looking forward. He minds about nothing else. And I mind about nothing else—'

For years after Lydgate remembered the impression produced in him by this involuntary appeal—this cry from soul to soul...But what could he say now except that he should see Mr. Casaubon again to-morrow? (MM 323-324).

Taken from its context, the second request, "Think what I can do," would have exactly the same sense as the first, "Tell me what I can do." That is, they are both requests for advice on how to alleviate Casaubon's condition. Dorothea's "Advise me," would suggest that this is, logically speaking, just what she is asking. This is therefore (apparently) advice which *anyone* under relevantly similar circumstances would ask for. The reasons for asking and advising are complementary—they presuppose a common goal. The means which Lydgate prescribes are amenable to evaluation by anyone suitably qualified, as being conducive or not to the goal. Asking for advice also presupposes that it can be given.

From this perspective however, Dorothea's "Advise me. Think what I can do," would be either senseless or repetitious. Repetitious because the answer has already been given to her first request, and senseless because it bids no answer, as Lydgate's reply might seem to indicate— "But what could he say now except that he should see Mr. Casaubon again tomorrow?" However, this shows that Dorothea's "request" has a different sense.

Dorothea is expressing a despair indicative of her concern for Casaubon and her commitment to helping him complete his life's work. Compare this with the first (actual) request, "Tell me what I can do." In the latter case, suppose Dorothea does certain things in accordance with the advice given. We may ask, as spectators, why she is doing these. She could reply, for instance, "The reason why I am not telling him is that I do not wish him to be anxious, for, given his condition, he would be harmed." This is no different from the professional advice that "Anyone in such and such a condition, ought not to be made anxious as this would most likely cause harm."

On the other hand, Dorothea's expression of concern is not subsumed under, nor derivable from, a similar standpoint. She cannot say, without an appreciable change of sense and distortion in meaning, that "The reason why I, Dorothea, am asking for advice is because I am expressing deep moral concern and commitment." Neither is it open for her to say, "And anyone else faced with a similar situation ought to do the same." She cannot say these things because to say them, or to hold that these are the principles and reasons under which her actions are subsumable, may not indicate moral sensibility, but perhaps quite the opposite, i.e. that she is arrogant, or not genuine.

The sense in which it is possible for us to say that moral considerations have an importance for her, shows itself precisely in her expression—an utterance which, even if no one were present, "would have turned into a prayer." The perspective from which she views the situation therefore, is personal, for no one can solve her "problem" for her. That is why Lydgate's helpless response, "But what could he say now except that he should see Mr. Casaubon again to-morrow?", is such an eloquent one.

# Notes

1 I have adapted some remarks here from Simone Weil's essay, *The Iliad: or The Poem of Force*, translated by Mary McCarthy (Iowa City: The Stone Wall Press, 1973).

2 See Lawrence Stern, "Freedom, Blame, and Moral Community," *The Journal of Philosophy* 71 (1974), for a similar point, though not in relation to Rosamond. Stern comments on P.F. Strawson's "Freedom and Resentment," in Strawson's *Freedom and Resentment* (London: Methuen, 1974).

# Chapter Six

## Perspectives and Moral Resolution

This chapter discusses a moral dilemma facing Dorothea, in *Middlemarch*. As spectators we may be tempted to say that there is an obvious solution which any rational person, including Dorothea, should adopt. The reasons I shall adduce for resisting this conclusion shall clarify the sense of a "perspective" under which Dorothea acts. The clarification proceeds further through a critique of Richard Brandt's theory of "cognitive psychotherapy"[1] and Thomas Nagel's "view from nowhere."[2]

### Perspectives on a Dilemma

Casaubon is seriously ill and has asked Dorothea to complete his work, a *Key to all Mythologies*, after his death. Dorothea is under no illusion that the work is of any worth. It would be an enormous burden if she promises. She goes through the following struggle:

And here Dorothea's pity turned from her own future to her husband's past—nay, to his hard present struggle with a lot which had grown out of that past: the lonely labour, the ambition breathing hardly under the pressure of self-distrust; the goal receding, and the heavier limbs; and now at last the sword visibly trembling above him! And had she not wished to marry him that she might help him in his life's labour?—But she had thought the work was to be something greater, which she could serve in devoutly for its own sake. Was it right, even to soothe his grief—would it be possible, even if she promised—to work as in a treadmill fruitlessly?

And yet, could she deny him? Could she say, 'I refuse to content this pining hunger?' It would be refusing to do for him dead, what she was almost sure to do for him living. If he lived, as Lydgate had said he might, for fifteen years or more, her life would certainly be spent in helping and obeying him.

Still, there was a deep difference between that devotion to the living, and that indefinite promise of devotion to the dead....

And now, if she were to say, 'No! If you die, I will put no finger to your work'—it seemed as if she would be crushing that bruised heart.

For four hours Dorothea lay in this conflict, till she felt ill and bewildered, unable to resolve, praying mutely. (MM 520-521).

Dorothea finally resolves to promise although Casaubon dies before she is able to do so. Nevertheless, it seems obvious that even if she had actually promised, she should not be expected to carry it through. This "obvious" solution can be stated impersonally as available to anyone in such a situation. Two questions are pertinent in evaluating the status of this solution. First, what is the relation between promiser and promisee? Second, what are the principles involved in the proposed solution, and is there some other perspective at work here?

The first question suggests that not anyone is in a position to promise, for some kind of relation must already exist. Therefore the solution of breaking the promise is not so obvious. Dorothea was already helping Casaubon and his implicit trust is not to be taken lightly even if the project is of doubtful value. A refusal to promise (sincerely) would mean abandoning him. This is clear if we note that Dorothea's perspective is not based on rights, i.e., that Casaubon is not entitled to her help and he has no right to ask in the first place. The person who holds this perspective of the relationship (as rights-based) may well think that after the death of the promisee, there would cease to be a bearer of rights, and as such, no obligation remains. But given the relation of trust as Dorothea sees it, this is untenable. As A.I. Melden has noted in another context, the commitment which one has made, in situations of this nature, can possibly remain "a moral burden one cannot slough off without loss of self-respect, even though the dying man ceases to exist and there is no longer the bearer of any right."[3]

The basis of Dorothea's (resolve to) promise is illustrated by how the obligation drops off after his death. She learns that he had added a codicil to his will, that she would lose her inheritance of his property were she to marry Will Ladislaw. To Dorothea, this cheapens the relation of trust and loosens the grip of duty:

Everything was changing its aspect: her husband's conduct, her own duteous feeling towards him...One change terrified her as if it had been a sin; it was a violent shock of repulsion from her departed husband, who had had hidden thoughts, perhaps perverting everything she said and did.... (MM 532).

But he had come...to create a trust for himself out of Dorothea's nature: she could do what she resolved to do: and he willingly imagined her toiling under the fetters of a promise to erect a tomb with his name upon it...The grasp had slipped away...now her judgment, instead of being controlled by duteous devotion, was made active by the imbittering discovery that in her past union there had lurked the hidden alienation of secrecy and suspicion. (MM 535).

The second question mentioned above suggests that there is another perspective behind the proposed solution which contrasts with Dorothea's. Thus the following syllogisms may be relevant:

(1) Anyone ought to prevent suffering (which might lead to death).
    This act of promising will prevent suffering.
    Therefore one ought to promise.

(2) No one is obliged to carry on a worthless task of another's after his death.
    This particular task is, by all accounts, worthless.
    Therefore one is under no obligation to carry on the task, and should not promise.

It might be said that a rational agent would put more weight on (1) than (2). An important consideration is the risk of the promisee's death should one refuse to promise. Preventing this has priority over not burdening oneself. In any case, one could subsequently break the promise. This is sanctioned by the general principle in syllogism (2). All things considered, therefore, one should promise.

It is clear that Dorothea does not give any weight to the possibility of breaking the promise because of her commitment to Casaubon. The question is whether she is irrational in discounting this possibility. What leads to the proposed solution and underlies its rationality is the perception that Dorothea is not obliged to do what Casaubon asks. In other words, syllogism (2) is just as important as syllogism (1), if not more so. The decision to promise is based on this thought: "One is not obliged to promise, indeed, it is unreasonable to expect it. But since there is a risk of worsening his condition if one refuses, one should promise. Of course, one isn't really promising, since one may not carry through the promise."

The proposed solution is "rational," therefore, given the rights-based perception that there is no obligation, and that one may simply go through the motions of promising. As we have seen, this is not Dorothea's perception and there is no general conception of rationality which necessarily governs the way she perceives, or should perceive, the situation. The perception that one is not obliged to promise does not constitute such a general conception of rationality. Instead, it *is* a different perspective. Someone in a relevantly similar situation may hold this different perspective. What she cannot claim is that the solution to which it leads is more rational, independently of the perspective.

In reply, it could be argued that we have not considered the possibility of some theory of rationality which would give us an independent account. Dorothea herself comes to break her (resolve to) promise, on the basis of new information about Casaubon. This shows that she was not fully informed. Her action was, in this sense, irrational.[4]

**Cognitive Psychotherapy**

This is reminiscent of Richard Brandt's theory of cognitive psychotherapy which characterizes rational desires and actions as those which "survive maximal criticism and correction by facts and logic." (TGR 10).[5] Someone's action is rational, to a first approximation, "if and only if it is what he would have done if all the mechanisms determining action except for his desires and aversions (which are taken as they are)—that is, the *cognitive inputs* influencing decision/action—had been optimal as far as possible." (TGR 11). And a desire or aversion is rational "if and only if it is what it would have been had the person undergone *cognitive psychotherapy*." Finally, an action is *fully* rational "if and only if the desires and aversions which are involved in the action are rational, and if the condition is met for rationality to a first approximation." (TGR 11).

A decision to act is irrational if it leaves out some relevant piece of information which, if known, would not have led one to make that decision. For example, an academic deciding where to spend his sabbatical "overlooks the (possible) fact that a duplicate non-circulating set of periodicals important for his project exists in Berkeley but not at Stanford. If he had remembered this fact at the time of his decision, he would have chosen Berkeley without a doubt. Obviously his action was irrational in the sense explained." (TGR 11). The following is given as an example of cognitive psychotherapy: A small boy refuses to play with a neighbor because she is devoted to a pet rabbit, and he has an intense aversion to rabbits because someone once produced a loud noise in his vicinity while he was about to touch one. Suppose that the boy would be "disabused of his aversion if he repeated to himself, on a number of occasions and with utter conviction, some justified statement as 'There is no connection between rabbits and loud noises; rabbits are just friendly little beasts.' In this case his aversion would have been removed by cognitive psychotherapy and I shall say his aversion is irrational." (TGR 12).

Although there is a more extended discussion, the model of rational criticism is essentially as just described. Thus, desires may be mistaken in the following ways: they may depend on false beliefs, they may be "artificial"—aroused through the influence of the attitudes and values of others,[6] they may be a generalization from untypical examples—as in the case of the boy averse to rabbits, or they may have an "exaggerated valence" as a result of early deprivation—e.g. some people may have an insatiable craving for attention because of early deprivation. (TGR chapter 6).

Quite clearly, cognitive psychotherapy gives a causal, explanatory account of the genesis of desires. As Brandt says, "I shall show that desires/aversions produced in these ways are bound to extinguish by repeated self-stimulation by information, given the facts about how desires (etc.) extinguish as described...The procedure will therefore be deductive; it will be like showing how a physical particle of a given description must move under specified conditions, given what we know of gravitational attraction, electromagnetism, and the theory of motion under forces." (TGR 114).

On Brandt's account, as we have seen, a rational desire is one which survives cognitive psychotherapy. But, as Derek Parfit notes (echoing Hume), one could still have a preference, after being cognizant of the facts and thinking clearly, for the world's destruction rather than the scratching of one's finger. The retort that such a desire would not survive cognitive psychotherapy begs the question of what *is* rational.[7]

Another criticism is that a causal explanation of one's desires does not justify having them.  What makes them rational or irrational is soundness of reasons or quality of evidence for the beliefs attendant upon these desires.  These reasons and evidence provide grounds for our beliefs, independently of cognitive psychotherapy.[8]

But in this regard, note Brandt's peculiar sense of "irrational."  Certain desires may be misplaced or mistaken, but not irrational.  For example, if I desire that harm should come to the object of my jealousy, and it turns out that the man I suspected of being my girlfriend's lover is, in fact, her brother, my original desire is hardly irrational.  It would be irrational only if it persisted after its cause, my jealousy, was shown to be groundless.

Similarly for actions.  Referring to the academic who decides where to spend his sabbatical, Brandt states (above), "Obviously his action was irrational in the sense explained."  But this is odd.  Although his decision was not optimal because it left out some relevant piece of information, there is nothing irrational about his decision or action.  It would be reasonable to say that he made a mistake, not that he made an irrational decision, or acted irrationally.

How might cognitive psychotherapy apply to Dorothea?  As in the example of the academic, the most one can say is that she made a mistake, not that she was irrational or acted irrationally.  More important, however, is the fact that the theory cannot properly account for moral growth.

Central to cognitive psychotherapy is the emphasis on correcting desires through the application of facts and logic.  The following examples illustrate this concern.  I believe that an object, x, is another, y, and I desire y.  I go for x, in the (mistaken) belief that it is y.  For example, I bite a cookie and learn that it is an extremely hard cookie for dogs.  We may modify the example to illustrate a logical mistake.  Thus, a child who has no concept of dog cookies might believe that there is no distinction between cookie x and cookie y, believing that they are both instances of the same thing.  Learning from one's mistake is to learn a new fact and a new conceptual relation.  In both cases, one comes to appreciate the object for what (one now learns) it is.

Consider how we may apply this analysis to Dorothea's mistake about the parishioners of Lowick.[9]  In what sense is she misinformed?  Her mistake may be described like this:  she desires to perform acts of charity in Lowick.  She is, however, wrong about the poverty of the parishioners and thus also wrong about the means to satisfy her desire.  Discovering her mistake, she thinks of new duties in other directions.

But Dorothea's situation is considerably more complex, given the possibility of confused motives, self-deception and moral growth. A cognitive theory like Brandt's, if it is not to be confined to the level of analysis just given above, must provide some account of how Dorothea comes to recognize, for instance, that she is deceiving herself and how this leads to moral growth. As described by Brandt, cognitive psychotherapy should clear Dorothea of her confused motives by giving a causal account of the genesis of her complex desires, e.g. for moral, spiritual and intellectual perfection.[10] Once she is cognitively aware of the origin of these desires, she will come to disentangle the various motives and direct her desire to do good in the right direction.

Such a causal account is available to us, as readers or spectators. Thus, following George Eliot, it might go like this: She has a nature which is "altogether ardent, theoretic, and intellectually consequent." This is, however, hemmed in by a restricted provincial social life which seems petty and leads nowhere. (MM 51). She yearns for something "by which her life might be filled with action at once rational and ardent." (MM 112). Knowledge would enable her not only to gain wider vistas but also give her a theoretical and practical basis for helping others in a grand way. Not only is she mistaken that Casaubon would give her all this, but this grand conception serves as the center of her relation to others. She either treats others contemptuously if they fall short of the ideal, or uses them as a means to fulfilling her own ambition of becoming learned.

But as we have seen, there is reason to doubt the effectiveness of cognitive psychotherapy. Suppose that Dorothea becomes aware of the origins of her desires. Even if this allows her to disentangle her motives, it provides no reason to believe that she would turn toward doing good in the right direction. Much depends on whether she is ready to accept certain moral criticisms. Her acceptance of these constitute a *moral* discovery. Causal knowledge does not necessarily bring about such a discovery because she may not relate to it morally.

Cognitive knowledge does not come with intrinsic moral properties. Whether pieces of information are morally relevant or not depend on their being represented in a particular way, according to a certain perspective. Of course, not just anything can intelligibly count as a moral reason, and there are limits to what can count as a moral perspective. But in certain central cases of the moral life, we can justifiably say, the agent constitutes such a perspective. As such, he or she is not deploying reasons for action as if they are available to any spectator, and any reason adduced cannot

be fully understood without reference to the perspective against which
they may be held.  We have already seen how this is so, in the case of
Dorothea.  Where Dorothea is faced with a moral problem, for instance,
someone else may see none.  And it is not what Dorothea sees as a
spectator that helps her decide what to do.  Instead, it is *how* she sees the
situation that is important.

There is a splendid passage in *Middlemarch* which describes this.
Dorothea had chanced upon Rosamond and Will (whom she has come to
love) in a seemingly intimate moment.  She struggles through her grief
and reminds herself that she is not the only sufferer, and that she had
started on a mission to help others, i.e. to inform Rosamond about
Lydgate's innocence.  She comes to a resolution, that "The objects of her
rescue were not to be sought by her fancy:  they were chosen for her."
Following this, George Eliot narrates:

> She opened her curtains, and looked out towards the bit of road
> that lay in view, with fields beyond, outside the entrance-gates.
> On the road there was a man with a bundle on his back and a
> woman carrying her baby; in the field she could see figures
> moving—perhaps the shepherd with his dog.  Far off in the
> bending sky was the pearly light; and she felt the largeness of the
> world and the manifold wakings of men to labour and endurance.
> She was a part of that involuntray, palpitating life, and could
> neither look out on it from her luxurious shelter as a mere
> spectator, nor hide her eyes in selfish complaining.  (MM 846).

Clearly, this is not a description of *what* Dorothea sees.  A difficulty for
the cognitive account would be to specify what she desires, and what
might constitute a "reason for action" here.  Relatedly, what is "the object
of desire?"  I do not think there can be any specification of an object here
without reference to a perspective, which is precisely what the passage
describes.

## The View from Nowhere

In the passage just quoted, Dorothea detaches herself from her own
desires, and sees herself as one person among others.  She thinks that it
would be selfish of her to complain and look on the suffering of others
as a mere spectator.  This detachment has nothing to do with what
Thomas Nagel has implied as a perspectiveless view of the world, in the

title of his book, *The View From Nowhere.*[11] Instead, it is embedded within the personal history of a moral development, and not a view from nowhere.    Without a narrative of her personal history and moral development, Dorothea's detachment would be unintelligible. But this is precisely what Nagel's "view from nowhere" amounts to—it does not merely refer to what is ordinarily recognizable, as taking a reflective stance.  Instead, it has a metaphysical basis of detaching the self from the body, as "an austere universal self," (VN 63) looking in upon one's body as merely one item in the world.

This detachment comes about in the following way.  Nagel begins by referring to the "semantic diagnosis" (VN 57-60) that first- and third-person statements bear the same content.  This is so, even allowing for the fact that indexicals have an ineliminable role to play, such that first-person statements do not bear the same sense as their third-person counterparts.[12]  According to the semantic view, however, this is trivial, since the truth-conditions of the first-person statements can be impersonally stated.  Nagel's opinion, however, is that "the elimination of this first-person thought in favor of its impersonal truth-conditions leaves a significant gap in our conception of the world." (VN 59). Claiming that there is a significant content in the thought, for instance, that "I am TN," Nagel attempts to fill the gap by relocating the "I" outside the world.  This relocation is prompted by the philosophical thought:  How is it that "I can be anything so specific as a particular person at all (TN as it happens)?"  This thought is open to anyone, and not just to TN.  And it opens up the sense that there seems to be an arbitrariness to one's being a publicly identifiable person, with a particular identity—one could just as well have occupied another person or have had another perspective.  At the same time, however, one's identity cannot be accidental—the real me cannot in this way be the publicly identifiable person.   Hence, my exact location has to be determined.  A relocation away from the publicly identifiable person has to take place:

> Essentially I have no particular point of view at all, but apprehend the world as centerless.  As it happens, I ordinarily view the world from a certain vantage point, using the eyes, the person, the daily life of TN as a kind of window.  But the experiences and the perspective of TN with which I am directly presented are not the point of view of the true self, for the true self has no point of view and includes in its conception of the centerless world TN and his

perspective among the contents of that world. It is this aspect of the self which is in question when I look at the world as a whole and ask, "How can TN be me?" "How can I be TN?" And it is what gives the self-locating philosophical thought its peculiar content. (VN 61).

If Dorothea is to be said to have a detached perspective, it is *she* who has this perspective. It is unintelligible, on the other hand, to suggest that it is a "true," "universal" or "objective" self (VN 60-66) which has this perspective, and not Dorothea, who, on this metaphysical view, is a mere "window" upon the world. This metaphysical underpinning plays no role in any conception of objective reasons. We understand what they are and the role that they play only in relation to certain socially embedded and personal contexts. The concept of a universal self serves to obscure rather than illuminate their application.

It is worth noting that a similar obscurity underlies *The Possibility of Altruism*,[13] Nagel's earlier work. There, he argues that in order to see oneself as merely one person among others, one must be able to conceive oneself impersonally, as merely "someone." This entails a commitment to the impersonal standpoint. At the same time, this is (implicitly) a *criterion* for avoiding solipsism:

> All of our personal judgments, including first-person psychological claims, commit us to corresponding impersonal judgments about the same circumstances, viewed impersonally. *Otherwise* it would be impossible to apply the operative concepts to others in the same sense, and the *supposition* that there are other persons like oneself would be unintelligible. (Italics mine).[14]

Although he claims to follow Wittgenstein in his brief discussion of the difficulties and consequences facing the person who says that he knows what "pain" is only from his own case, clearly, Nagel has failed to appreciate Wittgenstein's remark that "My attitude towards him is an attitude towards a soul. I am not of the *opinion* that he has a soul."[15] In other words, Nagel's treatment of the conception of oneself as one person among others is misconceived. Denial of it has nothing to do with one's *taking* or *believing* others to be objects, but with treating, regarding, and responding to others as objects.[16] The conception of oneself as merely one person among others is closely connected with the ethical notion of recognizing the reality of others. For instance, it has the function in certain contexts of pulling up someone who has behaved badly. It is an established part of moral language. Nagel goes wrong in attempting to give it a foundation, in terms of a criterion (for avoiding solipsism), which has no place in it.

Nagel has apparently ceased to be the Kantian impersonalist that he was in *The Possibility of Altruism*. This is because of his concession to "agent-relative" reasons, i.e. those which make an essential reference to the person holding them. In contrast to his earlier view, Nagel now argues that "the hegemony of neutral reasons and impersonal values is typically challenged by three broad types of reasons that are relative in form, and whose existence seems to be independent of impersonal values." (VN 165). These are (1) reasons of autonomy, stemming from desires, projects, commitments, and personal ties of the agent, giving him reasons to act in pursuit of his own ends, (2) deontological reasons, stemming from "the claims of others not to be maltreated in certain ways," being relative in that the agent requires himself not to act in these ways; and (3) reasons of obligation, referring to special obligations toward those to whom we are closely related, i.e. parents, children, spouses, siblings, fellow members of a community or even a nation. (VN 165).

Despite this concession, Nagel nonetheless uses the terms "objective" and "impersonal" to encompass both kinds of reasons.[17] This has a *reflective* application: from the objective/impersonal point of view, we may see the place for agent-relative reasons in our lives, and not distort them in neutral terms. There are other indications, however, that Nagel uses the objective/impersonal as a *justificatory* constraint for both agent-relative and agent-neutral reasons, in such a way that it no longer becomes clear that the former can be held independently of the latter.

Thus for Nagel it is the objective self, i.e. the self situated "nowhere," that must engage in practical reasoning. From this perspectiveless view, "the world of reasons, including my reasons, does not exist only from my own point of view. I am in a world whose character is to a certain extent independent of what I think, and if I have reasons to act it is because the person who I am has those reasons, in virtue of his condition and circumstances." (VN 140-141). For Nagel, the basic question of practical reason from which ethics begins is not "What shall I do?" but "What should this person do?" (VN 141).

Although Nagel recognizes that it may not always be appropriate to direct our lives from the objective viewpoint, and this viewpoint will not be a suitable replacement for the subjective, it will nonetheless "coexist with it, setting a standard with which the subjective is constrained not to clash. In deciding what to do, for example, we should not reach a result different from what we could decide objectively that that *person* should do—but need not arrive at the result in the same way from the two standpoints." (VN 155).

Against Nagel, given such a constraint, it is unclear how one "need not arrive at the result in the same way from the two standpoints." Consider the possibilities. First, both subjective and objective decisions may arrive at the same result coincidentally. Assuming that it is the same person who is trying to balance the two standpoints, this chance result is not what Nagel has in mind. The second possibility is where subjective considerations conflict with objective ones and the agent decides that the latter should overrule the former. But this example does not give us what we want either.

What we want is a third possibility where, presumably, the same objective result could be arrived at despite the fact that one is acting subjectively. If this is not to be a matter of chance, one would have to be aware of an objective decision procedure. Necessary conditions for arriving at the same result would be the following: (1) one is aware of what objectivity directs, (2) the result of acting subjectively should not clash with the objective result (despite the possibility of a clash), and (3) one's decision to act subjectively is dictated by objective grounds.

This third condition is inevitable, given the priority assigned to the objective standpoint. This is the conclusion to be drawn despite Nagel's recognition of agent-relative reasons. Nagel could reply that this is a misinterpretation of his view, which is that there should be the *possibility* of objective affirmation. "We should be *able* to view our lives from outside without extreme dissociation or distaste, and the extent to which we should live without considering the objective point of view or even any reasons at all is itself determined largely from that point of view." (VN 155). In other words, there is an objective standpoint from which one could appreciate the value of agent-relative reasons arising out of self-interest, autonomous projects and commitments, personal relations, etc., without claiming that they must be reducible to, or determined by, agent-neutral ones. One way of interpreting this is that in our reflective moments we could affirm the value of acting on personal reasons in various contexts.

But this reflective stance does not exhaust Nagel's position. Although he disputes the semantic diagnosis that first- and third-person statements bear the same sense, he does not seem to disagree that they share the same truth conditions. The relocation of "I" to a point outside the empirical self reinforces this idea, that first- and third-person statements have a similar objective content. However, we may resist this relocation, on the ground that this "perspectiveless" self is not, intelligibly, a true self because it has no narrative history and no character to which the individual can relate. Bringing the self back into its personal history, we may see how it is that first- and third-person statements may not necessarily be governed by the same truth conditions.

Certain remarks of Peter Winch's[18] are pertinent here. According to Winch, the relation of the moral agent to his action is not that of a spectator, who deploys reasons as if they are a guide to anyone wanting to make certain changes in the world. For taken like this, it is as if the moral agent is—like any spectator—looking upon himself or his body as one item in the world, subject to changes which he will effect through the justification of one set of reasons against another.[19]    Apart from discussing the limits to viewing morality as a guide to action (i.e. morality may instead serve as a kind of obstacle), Winch also draws attention to the fact that it is often important to see what the agent considers the alternatives to be, and the reasons he adduces in deciding between them.  Thus, two persons might be in identical situations and agree about what the issues are, yet decide differently.  But a more important difference is one where they cannot even agree in their descriptions of the situation and the issues raised by it—whether, for instance, the situation raises a moral issue or not.  Winch expresses this point by saying that "a situation, the issues which it raises and the kind of reason which is appropriate to a discussion of those issues, involve a certain perspective.  If I had to say shortly how I take the agent in the situation to be related to such a perspective I should say...that the agent *is* this perspective."  Winch is careful to add (contrary to  Sartre) that "the *possibility* of there being a certain perspective on a situation cannot be led back to any agent's choice. It depends on the language which is available, a language which is not any individual's invention...."[20]

The argument that impersonal truth conditions must govern first- and third-person statements assumes that an objective point of view necessarily governs the perspective of any agent, if he is fully rational. But this is to regard the agent as a spectator of his own actions.  I have tried to show, in the dilemma facing Dorothea, how it is that the "obvious" solution of the spectator is untenable for her.  Her relation to the situation is not what it may be for the spectator.  So too for another person in a relevantly similar position.  Where Dorothea sees a problem here, someone else may see none in the sense that she may think, for example, that she should merely go through the motions of promising.

As stated earlier, *what* the situation is, is not to be understood independently of the perspective of the person involved. This does not mean that there are no facts to the matter at hand or that one may take the facts any way one likes. For example, in the case we have considered, the fact that the promisee's condition is likely to be worsened if one does not promise cannot be ignored. But the relation of the agent to the facts can affect the status of those facts and the resolve to do one thing rather than another can, in itself, constitute a truth of the matter. Thus, for example, Dorothea's belief that she ought to promise (sincerely) can be presented imperatively,[21] i.e. she has no choice in the case and this constitutes a truth for her.

# Notes

1 Richard Brandt, *A Theory of the Good and the Right* (Oxford: Clarendon Press, 1979).

2 Thomas Nagel, *The View From Nowhere* (New York: Oxford University Press, 1986).

3 A.I. Melden, *Rights and Persons* (Oxford: Basil Blackwell, 1977), p. 51.

4 Another possible interpretation of Dorothea's action is that it is "supererogatory." Much discussion has revolved around this notion, stemming from J. O. Urmson's article, "Saints and Heroes," in *Essays in Moral Philosophy*, edited by A.I. Melden (Seattle: University of Washington Press, 1958). A paradigm example discussed by Urmson is a soldier throwing himself on a live grenade, thus saving his comrades (we may assume that he has just joined them and are not friends). But Dorothea's resolve to promise is the result of a personal moral history in relation to Casaubon. Acts of supererogation, in general, need have no such history, as in the grenade case. Such actions may, in a sense, be described as arbitrary or idiosyncratic—as has been characterized by David Heyd, "Moral Subjects, Freedom and Idiosyncrasy," in *Human Agency: Language, Duty and Value*, edited by J. Dancy, J.M.E. Moravcsik, and C.C.W. Taylor (Stanford: Stanford University Press, 1988). Heyd's use of the term "idiosyncrasy" is inapplicable to Dorothea's case. There is nothing idiosyncratic about Dorothea's resolve to promise, coming as it does from within the relationship with Casaubon.

5 Brandt, op. cit. Page references in parentheses, under the abbreviation, TGR. James Griffin, *Well-Being* (Oxford: Clarendon Press, 1986), also provides a cognitivist account of morality. But he prefers to use "informed" rather than "rational." Thus according to Griffin, p. 14, a desire is said to be informed when it is "formed by the appreciation of the nature of its object, and it includes anything necessary to achieve it."

6 The contentiousness of Brandt's ascriptions of mistaken desires is evident here. Why should the fact that my desires are influenced by the attitudes and values of others count negatively against them? I thank John Greenwood for raising this point.

7  Derek Parfit, *Reasons and Persons* (Oxford:    Oxford University Press, 1984), p. 118.

8  I thank John Kekes for the points in this and the next two paragraphs.

9  *Middlemarch*, p.103.  See a more detailed discussion of the example in chapter 4.

10  See Brandt, *A Theory of the Good and the Right*, chapter 6.   The example of Dorothea is, of course, supplied by me.

11  Thomas Nagel, op. cit.   Page references in parentheses, under the abbreviation, VN.

12  For instance, the thought that "I am ill" is not the thought that "X is ill."   This is especially so if it happens to be the case that I am amnesiac, and wrongly believe that "I am X."  I owe this example to John Williams.

13  Thomas Nagel, *The Possibility of Altruism* (Oxford:    Clarendon Press, 1970).  See chapter 11.

14  Ibid., p. 106.

15  Ludwig Wittgenstein, *Philosophical Investigations* (Oxford:  Basil Blackwell, 1968), Part II iv.

16  See remarks by L.R. Reinhardt, "Wittgenstein and Strawson on Other Minds," in *Studies in the Philosophy of Wittgenstein*, edited by Peter Winch (London:  Routledge and Kegan Paul, 1969), p. 164.

17  As noted by Blum, "Iris Murdoch and the Domain of the Moral," *Philosophical Studies* 50 (1986), p. 351.   This paper appears as chapter 2 of his book, *Moral Perception and Particularity* (Cambridge:  Cambridge University Press, 1994).  Blum refers to Nagel's Lecture on "The Limits of Objectivity," in *The Tanner Lectures on Human Value*, edited by Sterling McMurrin (Salt Lake City:  University of Utah Press, 1980).   On p. 102, Nagel remarks, "Both agent-relative and agent-neutral reasons are objective, since

both can be understood from outside the viewpoint of the individual who has them." But see also *The View From Nowhere*, pp. 172, 174, and 202.    Edward F. Mooney, in a review of *The View From Nowhere*, "Living with Double Vision: Objectivity, Subjectivity and Human Understanding," *Inquiry*, 31 (1988), discusses the several senses of "objectivity" as used by Nagel. See also Norman Malcolm, "Subjectivity," *Philosophy* 63 (1988).

18    Peter Winch, "Moral Integrity," in *Ethics and Action* (London: Routledge and Kegan Paul, 1972).

19    Ibid., pp. 171-172.

20    Ibid., p. 178.

21    In a critique of Philippa Foot's "Morality as a System of Hypothetical Imperatives," John McDowell talks of the categorical imperative in terms of the language of perception (what the virtuous man sees).   This seems to allow for a certain sense of necessity which although manifestly anti-Humean, is also non-Kantian. It is an Aristotelian position instead.    See McDowell, "Are Moral Requirements Hypothetical Imperatives?" *Proceedings of the Aristotelian Society*, Supplementary Volume LII (1978). I do not put forward the Dorothea example as a characterization of "the virtuous person," but instead to illustrate a sense of necessity to moral action which is subjective or personal.   I thank Mabel Eickemeyer for drawing my attention to McDowell's paper.

Interestingly, Bernard Williams has recently argued that the language of shame of the ancient Greeks, as portrayed by the Greek tragedians, brings with it a sense of necessity which, although it is non-hypothetical, is not captured in terms of the categorical imperative either.   Williams explains this in terms of the conception of an "internalised other" which "has some independent identity: that it is not just a screen for one's own ethical ideas but is the locus of some genuine social expectations."   The trouble with the Kantian picture of moral life, Williams argues, is that it seems to require a conception of the moral self which is "characterless."   See pp. 94 and 98 of Williams, *Shame and Necessity* (Berkeley:    University of California Press, 1993).

# Chapter Seven

## Nietzsche, Immoralism and Perspectives

The preceding chapters have discussed the possibility of various moral perspectives.  We should compare this with the idea that morality is *per se* a perspective, implying that there are no moral facts and no distinction between good and evil.

### Nietzsche and Immoralism

This is the interpretation of Nietzsche's "immoralism" put forward by Alexander Nehamas in his book, *Nietzsche: Life as Literature.*[1] According to Nehamas, Nietzsche holds a picture of morality as a system of values introduced by rulers wanting to perpetuate their rule.  This involves force, exploitation, and the perpetuation of certain myths which become ingrained in the psyche of the people.  History shows a recurrent pattern of the establishment of new states and societies with their own laws and values.  These changes are brought about through revolt against former rulers, putting into play drives and passions which manifest the will to power inherent in all life.  Once the new society is established, the same drives and passions which brought it into existence—an enterprising spirit, foolhardiness, vengefulness, craftiness, rapacity, and the lust to rule —are seen as a threat to stability and become branded as immoral.

Nehamas notes that Nietzsche's immoralism is actually a way of expressing the following philosophical views.  Essentially, there are no moral facts.  It is a contextual perspective which gives value (or disvalue) to the facts, as shown in particular by the value inversions of the drives and passions.  This means that the belief in moral absolutism is also an untruthful imposition.  This is the doctrine that "good and evil traits and actions are inherently distinct from one another and that their character does not depend on the character of those who manifest and engage in them on each particular occasion." (NLL 213).  This separation of actions from the agents who perform them eliminates differences between people, makes for equal treatment, and perpetuates the myth that actions are good and bad in themselves.

Against this, Nietzsche holds that evil features are necessary in a person, if he is to possess any good features at all.  This denies the unity of the virtues, according to which "having one virtue entails having the rest of them as well." (NLL 210). This may refer to the inevitable costs of being virtuous, i.e. that virtue means the repression and suppression of deep passions and desires. Thus, the cost of reining in one's ruthless desires is a deep malice against oneself and the world, while a dull rigidity is the price of refusing to do what one wants at whatever cost to others.[2]    But Nehamas thinks that there is a further "unsettling dimension" to Nietzsche's thought, for "sometimes Nietzsche writes that the passions we call evil are themselves the very passions that result in the best, greatest, and most admirable achievements." (NLL 210). Quoting Nietzsche's remarks that there are no moral facts, he draws the conclusion that according to Nietzsche, nothing is in any way good or evil. Nietzsche himself claims that his purpose is "to demonstrate the absolute homogeneity of all events and the application of moral distinctions as conditioned by perspective; to demonstrate how everything praised as moral is identical in essence with everything immoral." (NLL 211).[3]

It is undeniable that Nietzsche, as interpreted above, offers us valuable insights, e.g. that good and evil are not discrete, absolute qualities; that they cannot be prised apart from the agent; good and evil somehow enhance each other and the denial of the unity of the virtues suggests some of the complexities of the moral life.   One way to understand Nietzsche, therefore, is to highlight these aspects of character and their relation to action. The kind of person one is gives a sense and a spirit to *what* one does. In other words, what one is said to have done cannot be specified independently of perspective. Sometimes, this is interpreted as saying that there is no absolute "good in itself" or a "thing in itself."[4] Thus, according to Nietzsche, "an action in itself is perfectly devoid of value:   it all depends on *who* performs it." (NLL 214).[5]   This is consistent with some of my arguments about the importance of perspectives. Nonetheless, there are other interpretations. As Nehamas notes, "Nietzsche's exact conception of the relationship between good and evil features remains ultimately unsettled. Are these simply necessary for one another, or are they literally the same? His texts do not answer this question unequivocally." (NLL 219).

**Morality as Imposition**

One possible interpretation is this. The absolute homogeneity of all events, where everything moral is identical in essence with everything immoral, suggests that morality is *itself* a perspective. This in turn suggests that morality is a perspective which one need not share, and which may be dispensed with. This possibility is highlighted in the story of Michel, the narrator of *The Immoralist.*[6]

Michel's illness and recuperation leads to an exaltation of his senses and a heightened awareness of the will to live. This "recrudescence of life" leads to an association of health, beauty, and strength, with wilfulness and rebellion against all forms of social constraints. He compares himself to a palimpsest—he would have to erase the more recent text to discover the more precious ancient text hidden underneath. (IM 32). He begins to "systematically revile or suppress whatever [he] believed due merely to past education and to [his] early moral indoctrination," (IM 33) abandons any vestige of discipline and gradually descends into anarchy.

Although he does care enough for his ailing wife, Marceline, to travel with her (ostensibly to help her recuperate), he manifests a deep restlessness. Marceline is exhausted by the abrupt move from place to place and is even more wearied by the fear of what is in his mind:

'I see what it is,' she said to me one day, 'I understand your...doctrine—for that's what it is now, a doctrine. It may be beautiful,' and then she added in a lower tone, wistfully: 'but it eliminates the weak.'

'As it should,' I blurted out in spite of myself. (IM 94).

Despite his love and pity for her, he tells us that he "detest[s] sympathy; every infection is hidden within it; only the strong deserve sympathy." (IM 90). His pity is mixed with contempt—Marceline's illness has tainted her.

That this quasi-Nietzschean stance is born out of confusion is shown by Michel's thinking about honesty and sincerity. He believes that a moral value like honesty arises out of constraints. On the other hand, he does not consider sincerity a moral value, believing that it can be found only outside of moral constraints. Given that the lack of constraints is (so he thinks) best exemplified in the lives of thieves, poachers and vagabonds, it seems to him that each of these men's worst instincts is the most sincere. Yet he confesses that he cannot say what sincerity amounts to. (IM 99).

André Gide's picture of the immoralist is therefore not a happy one. Michel is not a model of clarity and strength but of confusion, disintegration and despair. This is clearly brought out at the end of the novel when after the death of Marceline, Michel appeals to his friends to take him away and give him some reason to live. He says, "I myself no longer know where to look. I may have liberated myself, but what does it matter? This useless freedom tortures me...When you first knew me, I had a great steadfastness of mind, and I know that's what makes real men—I have it no longer." (IM 107). He is reduced to whiling away the time, compulsively feeling the coolness of pebbles in his hand.

In contrast to Menalque and Zorba (see chapter 2), he lacks purpose. Given an assignment by the Colonial Ministry, Menalque is complimented by people for his "services to the nation," the very same people who had before reviled him for some "scandal." (IM 65). His confident sense of purpose makes him strong and he has the right to be impatient with social restrictions and to be contemptuous of others' feelings about him. Zorba, as we have seen, is admired both for his strength, for despising men, and yet "at the same time wanting to live and work with them."

Perhaps, as has been suggested, Michel is an imperfect[7] or a failed Nietzschean and there are more successful forms of immoralism—although there have rarely been anything more than hints and suggestions of what such a position would be like.[8] Certainly, however, Menalque and Zorba, as we have seen, are more compelling. If there is a sense in which they are immoralists, one should realize that they do not stand "outside" (the language of) morality.

The role of perspectives, I have argued, is important in morality. However, I would disagree with any conclusion that morality may be denied since it is itself a perspective. No doubt there are moral perspectives in the way that there are, say, economic perspectives, but this does not rule out a distinction between good and evil.

Morality can and undoubtedly does serve ideological purposes, e.g. in moral education. But it would be a poor moral education that does not enable the child to distinguish good from evil. There are various levels of complexity here and the extent to which the child is able to distinguish between good and evil depends on factors other than the fact that he is *taught* about good and evil. This is often overlooked by zealous advocates of moral education. One does not become a person of integrity, for example, through simply being taught *about* integrity in a moral education programme. The absorption in and serious dedication to an activity on the other hand, has much to do with developing integrity. Integrity cannot be imposed. Thus although morality and moral education *can* be an imposition (e.g. someone imbibes and acts on certain rules fearing the consequences of non-compliance) it *need not* be so.

To begin with, one needs to learn a moral language which is not one's invention but instead part and parcel of the customs, conventions, rituals, myths and traditions of one's society. One becomes a certain kind of person *through* the language one has. Thus, for example, one cannot become a Confucian gentleman without the moral language, concepts and rituals of Confucianism. This same language, on the other hand, may enable one to become a hypocritical Confucian gentleman. It would be more true to say of the latter that morality has been imposed and that he is acting on an ideology.[9]

The man who values the ideals that his moral language gives him, on the other hand, makes them his own. He has learnt to appreciate them through the various circumstances and activities of his life. This does not mean that there will be no tension and conflict between various commitments, ideals, conventions and wants. These tensions and conflicts are an integral part of an individual's life, not an encrustation or imposition of society on a (non-existent) pristine self.

## Conclusion: the Role of Perspectives

Here is a summary of the role that the notion of "perspectives" has played in this book. The moral theories I have discussed both restrict and distort various moral possibilities. Thus in chapter 2 a social definition of morality was given in terms of "the moral point of view." This imposed the moral limits and made it seem as if there was no other possible moral point of view. Against this, the examples of Menalque and Zorba indicate the scope and depth of various moral possibilities.

The constraints of rationality, instead of demonstrating the logical boundaries of morality, served to legitimize egoism. The example of Rosamond (chapters 3 and 5) describes the perspective of an egoist whose actions may nonetheless fall within the range of impersonal reasons for action. In describing the exploitative and insensitive nature of Rosamond's actions, we are criticizing it in *moral*, not rational terms.

The contrast of Dorothea (chapters 5 and 6) describes moral growth. Her concern for Casaubon comes about through a process in which she recognizes the possible corrupt nature of wanting to be morally and spiritually perfect. One point I have made in relation to Dorothea is that a moral decision to act in a certain way, in a particular situation, is not necessarily constrained by impersonal considerations. In other words, while I can understand how anyone in such a situation might act, it does not follow that where I am concerned, this is how *I* ought to act. How is this to be explained?

One way of expressing this possibility, as I have done, is to say that the agent "constitutes" a certain perspective, or even more radically, as Winch has put it, he *is* this perspective.[10] The objection to this locution may be that a person has many attributes—physical, mental, attitudinal, etc. He is, in other words, many things. To say that he is a perspective, on the other hand, is mysterious or unintelligible. Perhaps what is meant is that a person's "perspective" refers to some attitude or aspect of his character, which may be relevant to a decision.[11] In other words, given that one may (constitutionally) be unable to live with not performing a particular action, perhaps one should perform it. Thus, although Dorothea is under no obligation to promise (chapter 6), she would be conscience-stricken if she does not do so (sincerely). This would be one of the relevant facts, among others, to be taken into consideration.

My argument has been, however, that a person's perspective serves to evaluate the facts and is not a fact among others. The role of perspective was missing in Brandt's theory of cognitive psychotherapy (chapter 6) with its emphasis on approximations to complete information about the facts. No doubt knowing certain facts might have a bearing on how one should act. But at a certain stage, even when all the facts are in, they have to be construed in a certain way. This does not mean we can construe the facts any way we like. But it is a salient consideration that men of goodwill may yet see the significance of "similar" facts differently, disagree on what the issues are, and even see an issue where others may see none. This has implications not only where a *decision* to act is concerned but also where two (seemingly) identical *actions* are performed. As John Kekes has noted, "The actions of different people may have vastly different moral significance, because they may indicate different principles of mind and temper, that is, different moral perspectives."[12]

Kierkegaard adds a twist to the same point. Not only may two identical words and actions have different significance, two *opposite* words and actions may have the *same* significance.

As love itself is not to be seen (for that reason must one believe in it), neither is it unconditionally and directly to be known by any one expression.—There is no word in human language, not a single one, not the most sacred word, of which we could say: when a man uses this word, it is undoubtedly proved thereby that there is love in him. Rather, it is true that a word from one person can convince us that there is love in him and the opposite word from another can convince that there is love in him also. It is true that one and the same word can convince us that love dwells in the person who uttered it and not in another who nevertheless uttered the same word.—There is no deed, not a single one, not even the best, of which we dare to say unconditionally: he who does this thereby unconditionally demonstrates love. It depends on *how* the deed is done.[13]

The notion of a perspective means having a certain character and temper. It may also be taken to mean having certain commitments. Thus, to have a moral perspective may mean having a commitment to certain conventions, beliefs, ideals, and principles. These commitments are open to criticism. Our commitments might not cohere, they could be unrealistic in the light of social conditions, some of them may be defeasible, i.e. they may not be held as dearly as others with which they conflict, or we might come to see that some of them are shallow or delusory.[14]

Thus I do not deny that the commitments of a perspective are criticizable and open to change. There are, however, different processes of criticism and change.[15] I have argued against the model of moral criticism and change presented in terms of a rational, third person perspective integral to most of the moral theories I have discussed. Some possibilities of criticism and change are inherent in the psychological and motivational complexities of the examples presented. As described, these are also moral complexities. Thus, someone may give certain reasons why he does or should do something. Although these could manifest a real concern or commitment, there may be other (perhaps less noble) reasons involved. It may be difficult to disentangle the motives and perhaps impossible to do so. The agent himself may not be aware of the complexity and he could deceive himself as to what he really wants, or where his commitments lie. Alternatively, he may not have any commitment, being unsure about what he really wants. Circumstances may force and mold some people to a realization and decision about commitments and priorities. For others, on the other hand, life may go on in a muddled or uncentered way.

Instead of irrationality, various moral criticisms are possible here. Criticisms based purely on criteria of rationality miss the point. Like Ibsen's character Peer Gynt[16] when called upon to settle final accounts, such criticisms mistake the logical for the ethical point. Peer is informed by the Button Moulder (a kind of God's messenger) that because of certain defects in his nature (like a button that lacks a loop), he is to be melted into raw material, together with a great many others. Peer objects vehemently to this merging of his self—"like a speck within a completely irrelevant mass." The Button Moulder replies that there is really no need to make a fuss because "Up till now, you have *never* been yourself, so it's all the same if you die completely." Peer laughs this off as a logical mistake: "Do you mean that Peer Gynt has been somebody else?"[17] Peer's appeal to witnesses testifying to his identity does not help, for they answer that rather than being himself, he has lived according to the motto, "...to thyself be—Enough!"[18]   In desperation, Peer asks Solveig, the woman he had abandoned long ago, to solve the riddle, "Where has Peer Gynt been since last we met?" Solveig's reply: "In my faith, in my hope, and in my love."[19]   Too late, Peer discovers the mode and significance of the *ethical* self, which is not the logical self.

Ibsen's story has the form of a parable, and this constitutes a kind of moral criticism.   Philosophical theories about the rational basis of morality on the other hand, fail to give a purchase on criticism, given that the criteria of rationality put forward can be met by the very people against whom they are aimed.

# Notes

1 Alexander Nehamas, *Nietzsche: Life as Literature* (Cambridge, Massachusetts: Harvard University Press, 1985). See especially pp. 211-214. Page references in parentheses, as NLL.

2 In this sentence I have paraphrased Nehamas' quotation of Philippa Foot, "Moral Realism and Moral Dilemma," *Journal of Philosophy* 80 (1983), p. 397.

3 Nietzsche, *The Will to Power*, translated by Kaufmann and Hollingdale (New York: Vintage Press, 1968), section 272.

4 Maudemarie Clark, *Nietzsche on Truth and Philosophy* (Cambridge: Cambridge University Press, 1990), interprets Nietzsche as rejecting the Kantian "thing in itself" and foundational views.

5 *The Will to Power*, section 292.

6 André Gide, *The Immoralist*, translated by R. Howard (New York: Bantam Books, 1976). Page references in parentheses, as IM.

7 As suggested by Albert J. Guerard in his "Afterword" to the novel. See Gide, op. cit., p. 115. Guerard also suggests that the novel is about the development and self-discovery of a latent homosexuality.

8 The figure of the sneering, bold and brash Thrasymachus in Plato's *The Republic* comes to mind. His thesis that "justice is the advantage of the stronger" is reminiscent of Nietzsche's, that justice (morality) is an imposition of the stronger (the rulers). Socrates' questioning leads to another interpretation, that it does not pay to be just. Julia Annas refers to the first position as a "conventionalist" thesis, that justice has no real existence independent of institutions, while the second is "immoralism," which does not deny the independence of justice from institutions. See Julia Annas, *Introduction to Plato's Republic* (Oxford: Clarendon Press, 1981), pp. 36-37.

9 See *The Analects*, translated by D.C. Lau (Harmondsworth: Penguin, 1979), 11.26, where Confucius silently disapproves of some rigid moral answers of his disciples, given in terms of ritual formulae.

10 Peter Winch, *Ethics and Action* (London: Routledge and Kegan

Paul, 1972), p. 178.

11  This suggestion and the above objection were made by Robert Stecker, in conversation.

12  John Kekes, *Moral Tradition and Individuality* (Princeton, New Jersey:  Princeton University Press, 1989), pp. 175-176.

13  Søren Kierkegaard, *Works of Love*, translated by Howard Hong and Edna Hong (New York:  Harper and Row, 1962), p. 30.

14  These possibilities of criticism are discussed in John Kekes, ibid.

15  This is discussed by D.Z. Phillips, *Through a Darkening Glass* (Oxford:  Basil Blackwell, 1982).  See especially the Introduction, and chapter 2, "Allegiance and Change in Morality."  The notion of moral perspectives is also discussed in his "What Can We Expect from Ethics?" in Phillips, *Interventions in Ethics* (London: Macmillan, 1992).

16  Henrik Ibsen, *Peer Gynt*, translated by Peter Watts (Harmondsworth: Penguin, 1966), Act 5.

17  Ibid., p. 201.

18  Ibid., p. 206.

19  Ibid., p. 222.

# Bibliography

Annas, Julia. *Introduction to Plato's Republic.* Oxford: Clarendon Press, 1981.

Aristotle. *Nicomachean Ethics*, translated by J.A.K. Thomson. Harmondsworth: Penguin, revised edition, 1976.

Baier, Kurt. *The Moral Point of View.* Ithaca, New York: Cornell University Press, 1965.

Blum, Lawrence. *Friendship, Altruism and Morality.* London: Routledge and Kegan Paul, 1980.

_____. "Iris Murdoch and the Domain of the Moral." *Philosophical Studies* 50 (1986): 343-68.

_____. *Moral Perception and Particularity.* Cambridge: Cambridge University Press, 1994.

Brandt, Richard B. "Rationality, Egoism and Morality." *Journal of Philosophy* 69 (1972): 681-97.

_____. *A Theory of the Good and the Right.* Oxford: Clarendon Press, 1979.

_____. "Two Concepts of Utility." In *The Limits of Utilitarianism*, edited by H.B. Miller and W.H. Williams. Minneapolis: University of Minnesota Press, 1982.

Brock, Dan. "The Justification of Morality." *American Philosophical Quarterly* 14 (1977): 71-78.

Brunton, J.A. "Egoism and Morality." *The Philosophical Quarterly* 6 (1956): 289-303.

_____. "The Devil is not a Fool or Egoism Re-Visited." *American Philosophical Quarterly* 6 (1975): 321-30.

Butler, Joseph. *Butler's Sermons*, edited by W.R. Matthews. London: G. Bell and Sons Ltd., 1969.

Carlson, George. "Ethical Egoism Reconsidered." *American Philosophical Quarterly* 10 (1973): 25-33.

Chong, K.C. "Egoism, Desires and Friendship." *American Philosophical Quarterly* 21 (1984): 349-357.

_____. "Ethical Egoism and the Moral Point of View." *The Journal of Value Inquiry* 26 (1992): 23-36.

Clark, Maudemarie. *Nietzsche on Truth and Philosophy*. Cambridge: Cambridge University Press, 1990.

Davies, Colin. "Egoism and Consistency." *Australasian Journal of Philosophy* 53 (1975): 19-27.

Dawkins, R. *The Selfish Gene*. Oxford: Oxford University Press, 1976.

Eliot, George. *Middlemarch*. Harmondsworth: Penguin, 1976.

Emmons, Donald. "Refuting the Egoist." *The Personalist* 50 (1969): 309-19.

Foot, Philippa. "Morality as a System of Hypothetical Imperatives." In *Virtues and Vices*.

_____. *Virtues and Vices*. Berkeley: University of California Press, 1978.

_____. "Moral Realism and Moral Dilemma." *Journal of Philosophy* 80 (1983): 379-98.

Frankena, William. "Recent Conceptions of Morality." In *Morality and the Language of Conduct*, edited by Hector-Neri Castaneda and George Nakhnikian. Detroit: Wayne State University Press, 1965.

_____. "The Concept of Morality." In *The Definition of Morality*, edited by G. Wallace and A.D.M. Walker. London: Methuen, 1970.

_____. *Ethics*. (Second Edition). Englewood Cliffs, New Jersey: Prentice-Hall, 1973.

Frankfurt, H.G. "Freedom of the Will and the Concept of a Person." *Journal of Philosophy* 68 (1971): 5-20.

Freud, Sigmund. *Beyond the Pleasure Principle.* London: Hogarth Press, 1922.

Gauthier, David, ed. *Morality and Rational Self-Interest.* Englewood Cliffs, New Jersey: Prentice-Hall, 1970.

_____. *Morals by Agreement.* Oxford: Clarendon Press, 1986.

Gide, André. *The Immoralist,* translated by R. Howard. New York: Bantam Books, 1976.

Glasgow, W.D. "The Contradiction in Ethical Egoism." *Philosophical Studies* 19 (1968): 81-85.

_____. "Metaphysical Egoism." *Ratio* 12 (1970): 79-84.

Gould, Carol. "Plato, George Eliot and Moral Narcissism." *Philosophy and Literature* 14 (1990): 24-39.

Grice, G.R. *The Grounds of Moral Judgment.* Cambridge: Cambridge University Press, 1967.

Griffin, James. *Well-Being.* Oxford: Clarendon Press, 1986.

Hare, R.M. *The Language of Morals.* Oxford: Clarendon Press, 1952.

_____. *Freedom and Reason.* Oxford: Clarendon Press, 1963.

_____. *Moral Thinking.* Oxford: Clarendon Press, 1981.

Henberg, M.C. "George Eliot's Moral Realism." *Philosophy and Literature* 3 (1979): 20-28.

Heyd, David. "Moral Subjects, Freedom and Idiosyncrasy." In *Human Agency: Language, Duty and Value,* edited by J. Dancy, J.M.E. Moravcsik, and C.C.W. Taylor. Stanford: Stanford University Press, 1988.

Hobbes, Thomas. *Leviathan*, edited by Michael Oakeshott. Oxford: Basil Blackwell, 1955.

Holmes, Stephen. "The Secret History of Self-Interest." In *Beyond Self-Interest*, edited by Jane J. Mansbridge. Chicago: University of Chicago Press, 1990.

Hospers, John. "Baier and Medlin on Ethical Egoism." *Philosophical Studies* 12 (1961): 10-16.

_____. *Human Conduct*. New York: Harcourt Brace Jovanovich, 1972.

Hume, David. *A Treatise of Human Nature*, edited by L.A. Selby-Bigge. Oxford: Clarendon Press, 1960.

Ibsen, Henrik. *Peer Gynt*, translated by Peter Watts. Harmondsworth: Penguin, 1966.

Kalin, Jesse. "On Ethical Egoism." In *American Philosophical Quarterly Monograph Series, Monograph No. 1: Studies in Moral Philosophy*, edited by Nicholas Rescher. Oxford: Basil Blackwell, 1968.

_____. "In Defense of Ethical Egoism." In *Morality and Rational Self-Interest*, edited by David Gauthier.

_____. "Two Kinds of Moral Reasoning: Ethical Egoism as a Moral Theory." *Canadian Journal of Philosophy* 5 (1975): 323-56.

Kant, Immanuel. *Groundwork of the Metaphysic of Morals*, translated by H.J. Paton, as *The Moral Law*. London: Hutchinson and Co. Ltd., 1948.

Kazantzakis, Nikos. *Zorba the Greek*, translated by Carl Wildman. London: Faber and Faber, 1961.

Kekes, John. *Moral Tradition and Individuality*. Princeton, New Jersey: Princeton University Press, 1989.

_____. *The Morality of Pluralism*. Princeton, New Jersey: Princeton University Press, 1993.

Kierkegaard, Søren. *Works of Love*, translated by Howard Hong and Edna Hong. New York: Harper and Row, 1962.

Lagerspetz, Olli. "Dorothea and Casaubon." *Philosophy* 67 (1992): 211-32.

Lau, D.C., translated. *Confucius: The Analects*. Harmondsworth: Penguin, 1979.

MacIntyre, Alasdair. *After Virtue*. Notre Dame, Indiana: University of Notre Dame Press, 1984.

Malcolm, Norman. "Subjectivity." *Philosophy* 63 (1988): 147-60.

McDowell, John. "Are Moral Requirements Hypothetical Imperatives?" *Proceedings of the Aristotelian Society*. Supplementary Volume LII (1978): 13-29.

Medlin, Brian. "Ultimate Principles and Ethical Egoism." *Australasian Journal of Philosophy* 35 (1957). Also in *Morality and Rational Self-Interest*, edited by David Gauthier.

Melden, A.I. *Rights and Persons*. Oxford: Basil Blackwell, 1977.

Mooney, Edward F. "Living With Double Vision: Objectivity, Subjectivity and Human Understanding." *Inquiry* 31 (1988): 223-44.

Nagel, Thomas. *The Possibility of Altruism*. Oxford: Clarendon Press, 1970.

_____. "Moral Luck." In Thomas Nagel's *Mortal Questions*. Cambridge: Cambridge University Press, 1979.

_____. "The Limits of Objectivity." *The Tanner Lectures on Human Value*, edited by Sterling McMurrin. Salt Lake City: University of Utah Press, 1980.

_____. *The View From Nowhere*. New York: Oxford University Press, 1986.

Nehamas, Alexander. *Nietzsche: Life as Literature*. Cambridge, Massachusetts: Harvard University Press, 1985.

Nietzsche, Friedrich. *The Will to Power*, translated by W. Kaufmann and R.J. Hollingdale. New York: Vintage Press, 1968.

Overvold, Mark. "Self-Interest and the Concept of Self-Sacrifice." *Canadian Journal of Philosophy* 10 (1980): 105-18.

_____. "Self-Interest and Getting What You Want." In *The Limits of Utilitarianism*, edited by H.B. Miller and W.H. Williams. Minneapolis: University of Minnesota Press, 1982.

Parfit, Derek. *Reasons and Persons*. Oxford: Oxford University Press, 1984.

Paterson, R.W.K. *The Nihilistic Egoist, Max Stirner*. Oxford: Oxford University Press, 1971.

Phillips, D.Z. "Allegiance and Change in Morality." In D.Z. Phillips' *Through a Darkening Glass*. Oxford: Basil Blackwell, 1982.

_____. "What Can We Expect From Ethics?" In D.Z. Phillips' *Interventions in Ethics*. London: Macmillan, 1992.

Plato. *The Republic*, translated by Desmond Lee. Harmondsworth: Penguin, 1955.

Rachels, James. "Egoism and Moral Scepticism." In *Moral Philosophy: An Introduction*, edited by Jack Glickman. New York: St. Martin's Press, 1976. Also in *A New Introduction to Philosophy*, edited by S.M. Cahn. New York: Harper and Row, 1971.

Rawls, John. *A Theory of Justice*. Oxford: Oxford University Press, 1972.

Regis, Edward, Jr. "What is Ethical Egoism?" *Ethics* 91 (1980): 50-62.

Reinhardt, L.R. "Wittgenstein and Strawson on Other Minds." In *Studies in the Philosophy of Wittgenstein*, edited by Peter Winch.

London:  Routledge and Kegan Paul, 1969.

Rhees, Rush. *Without Answers*. London:  Routledge and Kegan Paul, 1969.

Sandel, Michael. *Liberalism and the Limits of Justice*. Cambridge: Cambridge University Press, 1982.

Sayre-McCord, Geoffrey. "Deception and Reasons to be Moral." *American Philosophical Quarterly* 26 (1989): 113-22.

Scruton, Roger. *Sexual Desire*. London:  Weidenfeld and Nicolson, 1986.

Skinner, B.F. *Beyond Freedom and Dignity*. London:  Jonathan Cape, 1972.

Stern, Lawrence. "Freedom, Blame, and Moral Community." *Journal of Philosophy* 71 (1974):  72-84.

Stocker, Michael. "The Schizophrenia of Modern Ethical Theories." *Journal of Philosophy* 73 (1976): 453-66.

Stocks, J.L. "Desire and Affection." In *The Limits of Purpose and Other Essays*. London:  Ernest Benn Ltd., 1932.  Also in the volume of Stocks' work edited by D.Z. Phillips, *Morality and Purpose*. London: Routledge and Kegan Paul, 1969.

Strawson, Peter F. "Freedom and Resentment." In Peter Strawson's *Freedom and Resentment*. London:  Methuen, 1974.

Urmson, J.O. "Saints and Heroes." In *Essays in Moral Philosophy*, edited by A.I. Melden. Seattle:  University of Washington Press, 1958.

van der Steen, Wim J. "Egoism and Altruism in Ethics: Dispensing with Spurious Generality." *The Journal of Value Inquiry* 29 (1995): 31-44.

Weil, Simone. *The Iliad:  or The Poem of Force*, translated by Mary

McCarthy. Iowa City: The Stone Wall Press, 1973.

Weston, Michael. *Morality and the Self.* Oxford: Basil Blackwell, 1975.

Williams, Bernard. "Egoism and Altruism." In Bernard Williams' *Problems of the Self.* Cambridge: Cambridge University Press, 1973.

_____. *Moral Luck.* Cambridge: Cambridge University Press, 1981.

_____. "Moral Luck." In *Moral Luck.*

_____. "Internal and External Reasons." In *Moral Luck.*

_____. *Ethics and the Limits of Philosophy.* London: Collins, 1985.

_____. *Shame and Necessity.* Berkeley: University of California Press, 1993.

Wilson, Edward O. *Sociobiology: The New Synthesis.* Cambridge, Massachusetts: Harvard University Press, 1975.

Winch, Peter. "Moral Integrity." In Peter Winch's *Ethics and Action.* London: Routledge and Kegan Paul, 1972.

Wittgenstein, Ludwig. *Philosophical Investigations.* Oxford: Basil Blackwell, 1968.

Wolf, Susan. "Moral Saints." *Journal of Philosophy* 79 (1982): 419-39.